Thinking about English

By the same author:

Inglorious Wordsworths
A Study of Some Transcendental Experiences in Childhood and Adolescence
(Hodder and Stoughton 1973)

The Unattended Moment
Excerpts from Autobiographies with Hints and Guesses
(SCM Press 1976)

Thinking about English

Michael Paffard

Ward Lock Educational

ISBN 0 7062 3807 9

First published 1978

Set in 11 on 13 Baskerville by Jubal Multiwrite Ltd, London SE13
and printed by Biddles Ltd, Guildford, Surrey
for Ward Lock Educational
116 Baker Street, W1M 2BB
A Member of the Pentos Group
Made in England

Contents

Acknowledgments vii
Introduction 1

SUBJECT AND TEACHER

1 What is English? 7
2 What is a specialist in English? 9
3 Is English a subject? 11
4 How has English as a subject developed? 13
5 One subject or two? 23
6 Are all teachers English teachers? 26

LANGUAGE

7 What is language? 33
8 What kind of language is English? 37
9 What is correct English? 41
10 Should children be taught standard English? 46
11 What are the basic skills and should we be anxious about standards? 49
12 What ought we to teach children about their own language? 54

LITERATURE

13 What is literature? 63
14 Why study literature? 70
15 Can literature be taught? 76
16 What kind of discipline does the study of literature involve? 83
17 Can literature be examined? 87
18 What is poetry and how is it different from prose? 93
19 By heart, by head or by rote? 101

IMAGINATION, CREATIVITY AND SELF-EXPRESSION

20 What is imagination? 107
21 Created creative? 116
22 What sort of self-expression? 125
Postscript 131
Index 140

Acknowledgments

Earlier versions of some of the material in this book have appeared in *English, The Use of English, Education for Teaching, Educational Research* and *Educational Review* but they have all been revised and rewritten. Inevitably my ideas on the questions I try to tackle have been shaped by many other writers on English and the teaching of English. My debt to them is great and probably often unconscious so that my bibliographies must stand as the only practicable form of acknowledgment. Similarly, the students and teachers with whom I have worked for twenty-five years have contributed much for which I am grateful: teaching is, thanks be, a reciprocal process. I am particularly indebted to my colleague Mick Saunders and to Geoffrey Hutchings for reading drafts of some chapters and for making a number of very helpful suggestions and also to Mrs R. Wilkes for her care in typing my manuscript.

Introduction

This book has been written mainly for students preparing to teach English in secondary schools or further education. It may be useful to teachers of younger children or foreign students as well but it does not deal specifically with the special problems of the initial stages of learning to speak, read or write English. It is not, in any case, a how-to-do-it book. There are several excellent ones already in print which do give practical advice about lessons, schemes of work, resources and so on. I am not primarily concerned with 'How, When and What' questions though I shall refer the reader to some of these useful books.

'English', as the name attached to a part of the school curriculum, does not denote a clearly defined subject with a standard informational content (though there are, of course, conventional ways of using the time available). Rather it refers to a complex of skills related, in the main, to the children's use of their own spoken and written language – skills which can be exercised and developed in an infinite variety of ways. That is an accurate but not an adequate way of describing it for English is concerned with more than the acquisition of measurable skills: it is concerned with the use of those skills, with the quality of self-knowledge and response to the world for which language is the means of discovery and understanding. Skills alone are never more than a means to an end.

What I have tried to do is to provide some historical perspective to current debates about the teaching of English, to ask some 'Why' questions about the sort of things that go on in English lessons and, more particularly, 'What-do-you-mean-by' questions about the things people say when you start discussing

English teaching with them. A good deal of attention has been paid to psycho- and socio-linguistic questions by people concerned with English teaching recently but a good deal less, I think, to questions of meaning. The attempt to do so may be temerarious, but I believe we should explore these difficult questions: What is language? What sort of a language is English? What is literature? How is poetry to be distinguished from prose? and so on, not merely for our own understanding as teachers but, at an appropriate level, with our pupils too. Many of these questions, if you pursue them at all obstinately, turn out to be very complex questions indeed and very often I shall only be able to provide notes about directions in which answers might be sought or tentatively suggest distinctions which it may be helpful to make. Ask any recently and highly qualified young graduate, 'What is X?' (the subject of his degree), 'Why study it?', 'What kind of discipline does the study of it demand?', and he will not make a very confident or convincing reply. He has been too engrossed by the trees to think much about the whole wood. But a restless or bored class will in effect be asking precisely these questions and when he wrestles with their lack of interest and inattention he needs this confidence and conviction as a basis for constructive thinking. And where conviction is lacking he needs the capacity to recognize and the courage to face his confusions.

Some readers will want to ask additional questions or different ones from those I have tried to sort out in the following chapters and their varying length is an indication of my doubtless idiosyncratic perception of their complexity and their relevance to teachers of English. Inevitably I shall generalize and, in doing so, reveal something of my own predilections and prejudices. To that extent the book is a personal statement and, though often tentative, not, I hope, so cautiously expressed that it fails to stimulate discussion. Between writing this and anyone reading it in print, my own views will have been modified and perceptions altered, or I hope so, for the debate is dynamic.

Teaching English, as I know well, is a fascinating involvement which can absorb all the best of one's resources of intellectual, emotional and imaginative energy. Responding to and stimulating young people's interest and the flow of their language, day by day, leaves little time or energy for systematic analysis of what one is doing. I have tried to step back a pace and provide a schema for reflection. My aim is to promote clarity particularly where it may not always be suspected that there is any lack of it. It is possible, therefore, that the book may also provide a useful framework for experienced teachers on in-service courses who are similarly trying to step back from the fray and take stock of their work. I hope so.

Subject and teacher

1 What is English?

The word 'English' which is, of course, primarily adjectival, meaning 'of England', when used as a noun came to mean the English language or rather the various dialects collectively spoken by the Angles and Saxons at least as early as Alfred's reign in the ninth century. Only as a verb meaning 'to render into (modern) English' is it properly sometimes written without a capital letter but this verbal use is now regarded as archaic or affected. Thus Chaucer englished Boethius, and Dryden and Pope englished Chaucer. Pope confidently expected that they in their turn would need englishing:

> Our sons their father's failing language see,
> And such as Chaucer is, shall Dryden be.

This reminds us that, like all living languages, English is constantly changing though changes between Pope's day and our own have been slower than they were in the preceding two hundred years: literacy and the dominance of the printed word tend to slow down the pace of change, particularly in the form of the written language. That living languages change and that the 'bad English' condemned by pedagogues in one generation often becomes accepted usage in the next are facts all English teachers should remember.

English is not only the first language of the forty five million inhabitants of England but of some three hundred million people spread over the world, twice as many as speak Russian or Spanish. It is second only to Mandarin Chinese in the number of its native speakers though globally far more widespread and important as an international *lingua franca*, a fact which tells much about our enterprising but often rapacious imperial past. The demand for persons qualified or unqualified to teach English as a foreign language is, seemingly, inexhaustible.

Despite the political problems and the nationalist passions that questions of language invariably arouse, it is much more likely to become the world language than any of the two and a half thousand other living languages or artificial ones like Esperanto or Volapuk. It is very likely that native English speakers will be able to rely on the rest of the world communicating with them in some semblance of their own language. If that makes them complacently unwilling to learn any language but their own, it will be folly, for there is much one will never understand about language without some basis for comparison.

English started as a collection of dialects and so it continues. Originally they were European dialects but now most of them belong to native speakers of English in America, Asia, Africa and Australasia. Britain has always had regional dialects within its own shores. For English teachers in Britain many problems arise from the fact that one of those regional dialects, that of the South-East Midlands, has acquired prestige and status at the expense of the others, as the name Standard English suggests. The accent with which Standard English is usually associated – Received Pronunciation – has similarly affected attitudes to other accents. Varieties of English have acquired social as well as merely regional connotations. More will be said about this contentious issue in chapter 9.

2 What is a specialist in English?

If you specialize at College or University in the study of history or philosophy you are being initiated into the ways of an historian or philosopher; with physics, of a physicist; with psychology, of a psychologist, and so on with all the other Arts and Science subjects. As a student of English, what can you call yourself or aspire to be?

The word 'Anglist' meaning 'one who has a scholarly knowledge of the English language, literature and culture' first appeared in 1888 (O.E.D. Supplement) but is by no means widely familiar. Even less so is Anglistics, 'the study of English language and literature' (1930). Both words appear to have originated on the continent and spread little farther. This lack of a common label for people who have studied it is symptomatic more of the heterogeneous nature of the subject than of its comparatively recent appearance in the Groves of Academe.

The don in an English department may not have too much difficulty in identifying himself as a literary historian, critic or theorist, or as a language specialist or, more precisely still, as a philologist or mediaeval dialectologist; as an expert on seventeenth-century homiletic or the Victorian novel. But the graduate product of his department who has followed a course comprising some 'pick'n'mix' combination of linguistic and literary studies may be supposed to have a smattering of some or all of these specialisms. He may have gone to University in the first place to indulge and refine his taste in literature and to that extent he is as much an aesthete as a scholar; he may have hoped (misguided fellow) that the University or College would seriously encourage his own attempts at creative writing and to that extent he is poet, novelist or dramatist *manqué*. He may, of course, have studied English in combination with some other subject or subjects and, today, with the strong feeling among the young that their studies should be 'relevant to modern life' (a notion that needs to be examined) his interest in literature may be sociological, political, historical or psychological rather than strictly literary. It is still unlikely, alas, that his studies will have given him much linguistic insight into the structure and varieties of modern English.

The English teacher then, was probably 'good at' English at school: he may be one of a small minority of ex-pupils whose interest in the subject survived the methods by which he was taught which gives them a dubious validity in his eyes. The chances are that his experience in higher education will have made him into a literary specialist rather than any kind of expert on the living language and into a reader rather than a writer; a reader, what is more, largely of authors long dead, a 'cemetery watchman' in Sartre's phrase. His training may have inclined him to look at life through fictions: 'They forget', says John Dixon of English specialists, 'the steady pressure on the writer himself to get out into the light of *things* and bring to all the concerns of common life a heart that watches and receives'. He needs, at least, to see clearly his own distortions in a plain mirror and reflect on them. His imagination must embrace a pupil's eye-view of himself and his subject. Even Geoffrey Willan's satirical slant may be salutary:

> English masters hav long hair red ties and weeds like wordsworth throw them into extatsies. They teach english e.g. migod you didn't ort to write a sentence like that molesworth.

3 Is English a subject?

It is a matter of dispute among philosophers whether knowledge is best thought of as a seamless coat which we divide into subjects largely arbitrarily for convenience or whether there are distinct forms of knowledge clearly differentiated one from another by characteristic concepts and logical structures, techniques of investigation and tests of truth. Even if one accepts as useful the distinctions made in the forms-of-thought argument, it is clear that the traditional subjects of the school curriculum do not correspond precisely to those forms of thought. The science subjects would all belong to the same category ('empirics'): geography would be an amalgam of social and physical sciences: English, French, Latin and so on would all find themselves split between 'symbolics' and 'esthetics' (I use the terminology of P.H. Phenix in *The Realms of Meaning* 1964) corresponding roughly to the familiar language /literature cleavage which has characterized and, some would say, bedevilled these subjects.

English is, paradoxically, both less and more than a subject. It is less than a subject in the sense that it is not primarily concerned to teach *about* language or literature or anything else. There is little in the way of an agreed body of information which has to be transmitted from teacher to learner and this is what makes many school English syllabuses such phoney documents. Old fashioned ones, often more honoured in the breach than the observance, unashamedly made out of formal grammar and the history of literature such a corpus of knowledge that could be taught and tested like other respectable academic subjects. But English is mainly concerned with doing rather than knowing, in a word, with skills (which makes it like physical education) and more particularly with skills of expression, communication, discovery and evaluation (which makes it even more like Art). Like them, too, it is concerned with personal growth and with our cultural heritage. It deals with levels of personal experience and the matrix of language from which all other specialist subject concerns develop. What makes it more than a subject then, is tied up with the nature of language, the immense complexity and variety of the purposes for which we use it, and the nature of literature, the immense variety and complexity of the human experience it can convey. Both language and literature serve the present but also encapsulate the past, the history and culture which is part of us and of which we are inescapably a part.

Textbooks have a place in English but perhaps a smaller place than in most other subjects because, as Edward Blishen has remarked, 'the vital material of English lessons is what the children say themselves, and what they can be led to say about what is near and real and immediade *to them*'. In one sense we all have similar needs for language since we are all social creatures; in another sense our needs are intensely personal and private as we are all unique individuals. Through language we have to structure reality, that is try to make sense of the 'buzzing, blooming confusion' of the world outside ourselves (William James uses 'confusion' in its strict sense of a fusing together); through language, too, we have to bring order and control to the internal world where the bewildering flux of our feelings would otherwise control us. Similarly, our needs for imaginative literature arise both from our common humanity and our unique place in it. English lessons responding to these truths will constantly oscillate between private and public, past and present, introverted and extraverted, business-like and playful, factual and fictional forms of utterance and between solitary and collective bouts in the intolerable wrestle with words and meanings.

4 How has English as a subject developed?

In the sixteenth century, Richard Mulcaster, headmaster of Merchant Taylors' School where Spenser was one of his pupils, was much ahead of his time in thinking English in no way naturally inferior to the classical languages and advocating that it be cherished and taught to boys before Latin. Like his older contemporaries, Sir Thomas Elyot and Roger Ascham, he set a good example by writing vigorously about the new Humanist education in the vernacular. His view gained support steadily but very slowly over the next three centuries.

In the Oxford English Dictionary Supplement, 1889 is the date of the first example of 'English' used to mean 'English language or literature as a School or University subject or examination'. True, the Oxford English School, the first in the country, was not founded until five years later in 1894 but I suspect earlier instances of the word in this sense could be found. At London University the first official English paper (for the Matriculation examination) was set in 1839 – an early milestone on the road. It was heavily linguistic and grammatical in flavour. How many of today's students would care to attempt to 'Explain the origin of the form of the preterite tense in English, and point out accurately its signification, distinguishing it from the Aorist'? In 1859, at London also, English literature of a strongly historical kind was admitted as part of the B.A. examinations and provincial universities founded in the second half of the century followed suit. Philological and other historical language studies, following the achievements of German scholarship, were already well established and regarded as intellectually taxing and therefore eminently respectable. Old English was taught in sixth forms and included in the Higher School Certificate as late as the mid-1920s.

In elementary schools at the turn of this century, 'English' often meant formal grammar and was timetabled separately from 'Reading' and 'Composition'; each might be taught by a different teacher. The syllabus might be further fragmented into 'Recitation', 'Spelling', 'Handwriting' and so on. In the secondary schools, the status of English was scarcely more secure than in the Universities. It was regarded as a peripheral subject and expressly excluded from the advertised curricula of many public schools as an effete option suitable for girls, perhaps, but calculated to weaken the fibre of young British manhood. In the Harrow of Winston Churchill's youth it was the last torture of dullards of whom he was regarded as one of the dullest. In 1904 the Board of Education in its Code of Regulations required all state secondary schools to include English language and literature in their courses on learning from their inspectors that it was commonly neglected. This was partly the delayed result of Arnold's impassioned advocacy of the humanizing effect of literature and partly due to the rigorously formal and accurate literacy expected by employers of young white-collar workers. It was felt that judiciously selected passages of literature could, perhaps, help to inculcate proper sentiments and that a detailed knowledge of grammar was the indispensable prerequisite of effective writing. The most popular poetry anthology was W.E. (England, my England) Henley's *Lyra Heroica* with its patriotic lays and the grammar was often additionally justified in terms of the transfer of training fallacy long after it had been exploded by psychologists like Thorndike. Still English remained the Cinderella of the curriculum: Inspectors frequently reported that periods allegedly for literature were in fact spent reading geography or history texts: 'correlation', as it was called, was as fashionable a notion in the first decade of the century as 'integration' is today and had similar attendant dangers for English.

There were, of course, notable exceptions but, by and large, 'grammar' and 'literature' dominated the syllabus for twenty years, and until the Second World War in many schools. The grammar was formal and Latin-based though gradually the emphasis changed from form to function, from parsing to clause analysis, as Jespersen routed Sonnenschein in the great debate between academic grammarians and Palser and Lewis began to replace Nesfield and Twentyman in classrooms. Literature meant analysing and paraphrasing passages of Chaucer and Shakespeare; following up classical allusions in Milton with the aid of formidable footnotes, memorizing much biographical information about writers and identifying up to fifty-seven varieties of figure of speech including Anacoluthon, Prosopopoeia and Epanorthosis. Composition meant either imitating the great essayists from Addison to Macaulay, with a distinct preference for the whimsicalities of Elia, or exercises in prosody or dubiously utilitarian tasks like composing a letter of hypothetical condolence to a hypothetically bereaved relative. It would be fascinating to know which relatives the young tended to bereave and of which relatives they were bereft!

The exceptions were teachers and writers like Edmund Holmes, Caldwell Cook, Dorothy Tudor Owen, George Sampson and Philip Hartog, who all believed children were capable of developing skill in handling their native language more naturally and creatively. The educational theorist who focused their beliefs in creativity and individual expressiveness into an impressive and coherent philosophy of education was Sir Percy Nunn whose *Education: Its Data and First Principles* of 1920 remained widely influential for over a quarter of a century and is still in print today. These 'advanced' ideas were sometimes accorded cautious approval in official publications like *The Teaching of English in England* (1921), the report of the 'Newbolt Committee' of which Sampson was a member, or the Board of Education's *Handbook of Suggestions for Teachers*. How far and how fast they influenced common practice in the classroom is another matter.

The grammar schools found in the caution of the 1921 Report, and particularly in its equivocations about the teaching of grammar, an excuse for changing very little. The classical influence on the teaching of literature remained strong and a thorough grounding in English grammar was thought indispensable for children learning classical or modern foreign languages even if some 'progressives' had cast doubts on its usefulness to writers of English. The form of the School Certificate English papers changed very little between the wars and, in many respects even down to 1960, despite its transformation into the GCE in 1951. A candidate of 1960 would hardly have been put out if confronted by a paper of 1920 or vice versa. It is difficult to apportion blame or distinguish cause from effect: was the *rigor mortis* in which the subject was locked for forty years in grammar and public schools the result of or the reason for the extreme conservatism of the examiners? A bit of each, no doubt. Of course there were always some good teachers who kept the subject alive for their fortunate pupils.

Despite the pressure of the scholarship exam on some forms, the elementary schools were less impervious to change, and swings in the pendulum of fashion in educational theory affected them more. The 1921 Report was followed by a spate of methods and course books by writers like E.A. Greening Lamborn and W.S. Tomkinson in which self-expression, imagination and 'the culture of the feelings' were given much prominence and large claims were sometimes made for children's creative abilities. Inevitably the reaction came and the late 1920s and early 1930s saw many restatements of the importance of grammar, of traditional exercises like 'reproduction' and of systematic practice in sentence construction and paragraph building. 'Psychology' is blamed for slack standards and an excessive faith in undisciplined self-expression and imagination. Predictably the grammar school-dominated IAAM and Association of Assistant Mistresses are the most dismally negative in calling for retrenchment and ridiculing faith in the expression of miniature selves who can have nothing significant to express.

At the same time, on the literary scene, the gushings of Georgian 'belles-lettrism' were being replaced by the new, astringent, professional criticism of I.A. Richards, T.S. Eliot, William Empson and F.R. Leavis. By the mid-1930s there begin to appear 'practical criticism' books for upper forms of which Denys Thompson's *Reading and Discrimination* of 1934 is the first and the best. However, the great majority of text books remain depressingly formal, thorough and humourless sets of Scholarship or School Certificate exercises and tests.

The whole history of English teaching is one of major and minor swings of the pendulum between the extremes of the Classical-imitative and the Romantic-expressive schools of thought; between the claims of social and vocational utility and personal self-fulfilment; between the need for accuracy and order, on the one hand, and for fluency and spontaneity on the other. Timid advances in practice are often swamped and confused by the backwash of the previous wave of enthusiasm among the theorists and innovators. These movements, which could doubtless be paralleled in the teaching of other subjects, reflect in part the oscillations in educational theory as a whole. There was progress between the wars but it often resembled the jerky reverberations of a freight train getting under way with a good deal of heat and noise generated between the forward and backward facing buffers.

The pattern of English teaching since the last war is the easiest to see for the evidence is all about us and many of us have been caught up in its cross currents, but it is for that reason the most difficult to evaluate with critical perspective and detachment. Knowledge of earlier periods rightly leads us to expect many anomalies and twists in the story and to be wary of generalizations. Extremes of conservative reaction and progressive experimentation may coexist in adjacent schools and even side by side in different classrooms of the same school. General practice, as always, has lagged well behind theory and the advice of inspectors, advisers and official reports. At conferences, courses, meetings and in the journals there is much preaching to the converted while the majority choose to remain oblivious and stick to their time-honoured ways. Senior elementary schools when they became modern schools had no model of secondary English teaching except that of the grammar schools and, before many realized that a dilute academic type of English course was unsuitable fare for most of their pupils, they were overtaken by comprehensive re-organization, the challenge of mixed-ability teaching, integrated studies and other disturbing innovations. Yet vitality and experimentation did bubble up from the best primary schools to affect non-examination work in some secondary schools and, despite the GCE, much of the most heartening preaching and practice has come from teachers with predominantly grammar school experience. The most modern practices based on ideas of creative expression and self-realization are, as we have seen, clearly foreshadowed in the earliest years of the century, but while examination-directed conservatism has been a continuous tradition, for the progressives there has been

> ... the fight to recover what has been lost
> And found and lost again and again.

It could be convincingly argued, I think, that the insights of Holmes and Caldwell Cook, Sampson and Ballard were firmly grasped after the war by at least a significant minority of practising teachers and have helped to form the dominant philosophy of English teaching since 1960. It only remains to indicate in a very few paragraphs the broad outline of that philosophy and some of the influences that have gone to shape it. More detailed scrutiny of some of its ideas and assumptions must wait until later sections of the book.

Firstly, studies of the development of language in young children have been important: the psychologist A.F. Watts's *The Language and Mental Development of Children* first published in 1944 influenced a whole generation of teachers. What he and his successors have emphasized is that children acquire language by imitation encouraged by adults and in response to a felt need for communication and expression. Gradually the idea has dawned that this remains true throughout their schooldays and that it is unprofitable to practise language skills in the artificial context of the textbook exercise and unreasonable to impose on them language structures in advance of their stage of intellectual development.

Secondly, linguistic science has underlined the primacy of the spoken language. It is not really surprising that this obvious truth is being assimilated very slowly for 'literacy' and 'education' have been almost synonymous terms since the Renaissance. The spoken word was accorded something like its true importance for the first time in a major educational report by Newsom (§ 49,330) in 1963 and by the end of that decade the new word 'oracy' had gained some currency among educationalists. Even the examination boards were beginning to tackle the problems of testing oral and aural competence, a field about which we still know little.

Another crucial spin-off from linguistic studies has been the final discrediting of the old formal Latin-based grammar. It has been an unconscionable time dying and teachers and textbooks can still be found intent on dinning into the heads of young secondary and even primary school children the parts of speech and irrelevancies of gender, case and mood in the face of all the research evidence that such knowledge gives them no useful skills. At least in external examinations it is now generally absent or, at most optional, whereas twenty-five years ago it was an important and obligatory element in virtually all of them. The old grammar was artificial and prescriptive; the new transformational or structural grammars are properly scientific and descriptive but there have already been skirmishes about whether and at what level they might usefully be taught in schools. It looks as if there may be a strong case for teaching elements of structure to older and abler pupils but, just because the new grammar is descriptive, it seems unlikely that a knowledge of it will be any more help to most pupils with their speech and writing than the old was. Their teachers, on the other hand, may have much to learn about the medium of their message and the language habits their pupils bring already formed to school.

A final casualty of linguistics has been the time-honoured notion that correctness to a universally applicable standard of Good or Queen's English is the desirable end of language work at school. Studies of the great varieties of dialects, 'registers' and 'styles' of language in fact used for our multifarious human purposes makes such a monolithic idea of 'good English' untenable. We are aware too, as never before, how the notion of Standard English has served to mark out social class distinctions with all the attendant attitudes.

It would be over-optimistic to think that these ideas of language and language development have won universal assent: there is plenty of depressing evidence to the contrary. There is also a real danger that teachers who feel insecure without a syllabus content of information which can be taught, memorized and tested in a straightforward manner will be tempted to forge out of modern linguistics new shackles to replace those of the old grammar.

Other strands in the current orthodoxy of English teaching are complex, intertwined and part of the fabric of life in post-war Britain with its far-reaching social changes. If we dipped quickly into major reports of the pre- and post-war periods, say Hadow (1926) and Spens (1938) and then Newsom (1963) and Plowden (1967), we should be left in no doubt that our whole approach to education has become increasingly child-centred. For English this has tended to mean that the essential material of lessons has become the pupil's experience and his own language for what is near and real and important to him rather than a taxonomy of skills to be mastered, a programme of information to be learnt or a corpus of literary texts to be studied. The pupil's right to choose what he should read, what topics to write about and how has been emphasized, though wise teachers know the limits beyond which their pupils cannot profitably handle freedom in these respects. In stressing the importance of language in helping the child to come to terms with himself and the world he lives in, the tendency has been to choose contemporary material which is manifestly relevant to that world. Projects such as explorations of the mass media have commended themselves to English teachers with a social-psychological slant to their thinking and also, for different reasons, to those influenced by F.R. Leavis and his disciples who have been outspokenly and persistently pessimistic about most aspects of modern mass culture ever since the beginning of *Scrutiny* in 1932. Less acceptable to the Leavisites has been a trend away from scaling the heights of the 'Great Tradition' in literature or even attempting its foothills – away, indeed, from fiction altogether and towards biography, travel and social documentary writing often of negligible literary merit dealing with 'problems' like race relations, war, old age, sexual morality and environmental pollution. The Social Studies slant to English has often been deplored as showing a loss of confidence in literary values: it may have its origin in anxieties about the future of democracy and the economic disasters of the 1930s.

The egalitarian spirit manifested in comprehensive reorganization has given a new clarity and sense of urgency to the cultural aspirations of Matthew Arnold and the 1921 Report: all children, regardless of their class background, their intelligence or their future work have the same human need for a language adequate for the great experiences of birth and death, love and hate, success and failure, joy and anguish, and the same right to realize their creative potential. In its more politically partisan forms this egalitarianism has sometimes led to the rejection of many fine books for children as 'middle class' or 'élitist' and to a search for the authentic voice of the working classes. Richard Hoggart's *The Uses of Literacy* (1957), often misunderstood and misrepresented, was influential in this connection.

Finally, since the war, there has been a change amounting to a revolution in attitudes to children's writing. Norman Morris's *First Fruits* (1939) was probably the first collection to appear between hard covers from a publisher but the contents were mainly exercises in literary pastiche. Recent years have seen a number of collections of writing freer in form and more authentically the children's own in language and preoccupation. Often the contents are impressive judged by any standard, though one suspects that the taste and talent of the teachers who stimulated, selected and perhaps helped to polish the work for publication may be more important than is always admitted.

High claims for the imaginative and aesthetic quality of children's painting were made between the wars by Franz Cizek and Wilhelm Viola on the continent and, later, by Herbert Read in England (*Education Through Art* 1943). Marjorie Hourd was one of the first since the 1920s and probably the most influential writer to revive similar claims for children's writing. Her book *The Education of the Poetic Spirit* appeared in 1949. The theory, as it has been developed by numerous subsequent writers, is strongly romantic in its underlying premises; it combines Coleridge's view of the centrality of the imagination and Wordsworth's faith in the child as 'Mighty Prophet! Seer blest!' with a twentieth century view of the unconscious as the source of inspiration to which the child may have readier access than the more self-conscious adult.

The criteria for judging children's work – in so far as the adult dares to judge it – are similarly romantic and subjective; spontaneity, imaginative involvement, intensity and honesty to first-hand experience are the qualities looked for. Creativity is seen as largely independent of intelligence, academic ability or general knowledge. Mechanical accuracy, it is felt, can be attended to at the proof-reading stage. Despite fairly frequent complaints from employers and others about the supposed decline in standards of spelling and punctuation, the general view has been that 'copiousness will in time secure accuracy', as P.B. Ballard put it as long ago as 1921, and it is generally agreed that, as Newsom says 'Teachers whose sole standard is correctness can dry up the flow of language and shackle creative and imaginative writing before it is under way' (§481). Writers like David Holbrook and Simon Stuart sometimes even seem to suggest that they value children's writing in proportion as it reveals a probing of psychic problems and serves as therapeutic to the writer so that the English teacher needs psycho-analytic rather than literary-critical skills to read his pupils' work. A similar suggestion is implicit in much writing by Peter Slade and others about child drama which has tended to become an independent 'subject' in which language is secondary to movement and a script or a stage are the last things a teacher requires.

This represents the crudest outline sketch of a complicated picture. All I have done is indicate some common ground of shared beliefs between, say, most of the writers in *The Use of English* since 1949 or between the teachers who attend the annual conferences of the National Association for the Teaching of English (founded in 1963). Of course, there have been voices of caution and contradiction: of course the less adventurous majority of teachers, as David Shayer wisely remarks, 'prefer to know exactly what they are supposed to be doing and are less happy when left free to find their own way, however beneficial such freedom can be to their pupils if put to thoughtful and imaginative use'. They tend to be the course-book buyers and many of the best selling course-books have remained solidly conservative and traditional in their contents. Even the more recent books and packs of open-ended stimulus material are not teacher-proof and can be used in stereotyped ways.

The problem for the teacher, now as at any time, is to combine the best innovations with tried and tested methods, a respect for the individuality and interests of the pupil with a proper regard for standards which are not fugitive. Pope's advice remains relevant:

> Be not the first by whom the new are tried,
> Nor yet the last to lay the old aside!

5 One subject or two?

At one time, as we have seen, aspects of English language such as grammar and English literature were often timetabled separately and even taught by different teachers. The GCE examination boards have perpetuated this separation of language and literature and it is common for candidates at O level to take one without the other. At A level the subject remains exclusively literary despite fifteen years of discussion of the desirability of an option in modern linguistics. In the universities, also, there often seems to be little common ground between those who profess the various linguistic sciences and those whose interests are in literary criticism and history. If they are essentially different disciplines at this level and, perhaps, with advanced students in school who have begun to specialize, it is at least arguable that they should be organized into separate syllabuses. It does not follow from this, however, that language and literature work should be separated at school level for the majority of children. Most school subjects show a similar progressive differentiation into distinct branches in higher education. Neither does it follow that students cannot profitably combine in their programme material from two or more disciplines. No one, I imagine, would deny that at a proper interdisciplinary level literary critics can gain valuable insights from linguists and vice versa. Nevertheless, linguistic scientists often speak of literature as just one rather specialized register of language which scarcely impinges on most people's lives and has, in any case, attracted a disproportionate amount of attention from scholars in the past. Literary critics on the other hand often regard the allegedly objective and value-free enquiries of linguists as remote from the study of literature as a human discipline of the sensibility and intelligence which is inescapably moral because, as F.R. Leavis has argued, 'it is inseparable from that profound sense of relative value which determines, or should determine, the important choices of actual life'.

This is obviously a complex and controversial question and it would be inappropriate to examine the arguments in detail here. However, it does seem worth suggesting some of the reasons why a unified rather than the old fragmented approach to English at school level makes best sense.

In the first place it would be odd to teach the use of English without studying the masters who have produced what is indisputably one of the great literatures of the world; literature is language, after all, even if very little language is literature.

Secondly and more specifically, if we assume for the moment that we should encourage children to write personally, creatively and imaginatively and not solely for utilitarian purposes, it would be absurd not to show them from suitable imaginative literature something of the marvellous possibilities of language. This is not to revive the old practice of requiring children to imitate the style of *Elegant Extracts* chosen from approved authors but it does recognize the fact that emulation of genuinely admired authors has played a part in the making of most good writers. As Archibald MacLeish puts it, 'A real writer learns from earlier writers the way a boy learns from an apple orchard – by stealing what he has a taste for and can carry off'.

Thirdly, literature will often provide the most vivid and challenging material to stimulate acting, debating, discussing and writing as well as all those non-linguistic activities which will help children to develop self-confidence and self-expressiveness. If English is about finding words for the children's experience of the world, literature introduces new voices and new vicarious experiences into that world as well as serving to confirm what is already there.

Finally, a study of the use of language today must include its use in advertising and all the more and less insidious forms of persuasion and propaganda. If the study of emotive language in propaganda is separated from the study of literature, children are very likely to be left with the impression that all emotive use of language is suspect and underhand. Many textbooks with a social studies slant fall into precisely this trap. C.S. Lewis has powerfully argued in *The Abolition of Man* that this encourages a facile, destructive rationalism and a smug cynicism ('Huh!

They can't fool me.') which can cut the ground from under our feet when we teach literature. We do not want to make children unfeeling or unresponsive to the emotive power of words but enable them to discriminate between ordinate and inordinate emotions, honest and dishonest uses of language. And so it is essential to put side by side language which legitimately seeks to persuade and expresses and arouses passions and language which seeks to exploit people through those passions for ulterior motives.

6 Are all teachers English teachers?

The Newbolt Report of 1921 said, 'It is impossible to teach any subject without teaching English'. The maxim that all teachers are teachers of English contains an important truth but oversimplifying a complex issue can lead to certain dangers. It is true that most teachers most of the time are using the native language and encouraging children to use it in the process of learning to be geographers, historians, scientists and so on. The quantity and quality of a pupil's knowledge and understanding in these subjects cannot be separated from the quantity and quality of appropriate language he has learnt to use in the process. In this sense most teachers must be concerned with their students' skill in using language for limited and specific purposes. What you know, what you say and how you say it are inextricably interrelated. They will be concerned with other skills as well: observing, measuring, calculating, analysing, dissecting: modern methods of teaching and testing are often less word-dominated than old-fashioned chalk-and-talk ones. In learning foreign languages by the 'direct' method the pupil may very properly be discouraged from using English at all; and in some subjects like mathematics, art and music which have their own symbolic systems or 'languages', they may be encouraged to use them rather than verbalizing their ideas and feelings. When anxieties about standards of literacy are expressed, the extent to which school learning (as well as leisure) has become less book-centred and verbal is seldom mentioned.

Nevertheless, for most purposes most of the time our native language is the medium in which we think, order, record and communicate our experience and manipulate our environment. This is why English is more than a subject, all teachers are – *faute de mieux* – English teachers and schools as a whole and not just the English departments within them need a concerted language policy as the Bullock Report has insisted.

Experience suggests that, if a pupil needs help in improving his lab reports, the place to help him most effectively is not in special remedial or 'service' English lessons but on the lab bench in the light of the purpose for which he is using the language (and so, *mutatis mutandis*, with other subjects too). This is not, of course, to say that there will be no place for remedial or general English lessons in a school. Another of the reasons why all teachers should be teachers of English and be seen to be so is that pupils might otherwise come to believe that they only need pay attention to their written and oral expression in lessons called English; that good English is something that can be turned on for the fussy English teacher and then turned off again. Children have to learn to adapt their language to the purposes and contexts in and for which they are using it, as will be stressed elsewhere, but not in this way.

Unfortunately there is a good deal of evidence now that most teachers are bad teachers of English at this general level and, hence, less effective teachers of their own subjects than they might be. In the spoken and written English they use and encourage, and in the textbooks they adopt the language is often a formal 'transactional' one with a technical vocabulary which is at best inappropriate to the children's level of intellectual development and at worst unintelligible. Otherwise dedicated and sensitive teachers often have little awareness of the barriers to comprehension and real learning that such language sets up. Children require, above all else, lots of talk at a much more expressive and informal level if new ideas and information are going to be grasped and made their own rather than learnt parrot-fashion. Insistence on a formal, impersonal style coupled with a censorious attitude to mistakes in the formal conventions of spelling, punctuation and grammar can undermine children's confidence in their own language as a powerful tool for understanding the world and communicating. English teachers, of course, as well as non-specialists can be insensitive about the language of the classroom in this way.

The dangers inherent in insisting that all teachers are English teachers then, are obvious. It may encourage the false assumption that all teachers are equally well able to understand the nature of language and children's language needs and difficulties. It may increase the common tendency for non-specialists to find some periods of English on their timetables regardless of their experience, qualifications and inclinations. The Bullock Report found that 'no fewer than a third of all secondary teachers engaged in the teaching of English have no qualification in the subject'. (Ch.I.II) It may undermine the place of English in the timetable and thus reduce the opportunity of pupils for the more personal and subjective aspects of expression in language and for experiencing literature which English lessons uniquely provide. It was represented to the Bullock Committee that when English is allowed to be swallowed up in integrated studies, 'The pupil's writing becomes narrow in range, with the factual predominating and the imaginative finding little place. Literature tends to be either neglected or bent to conform with the dictates of other components.' (Ch.I5.4)

Ideally children should use English intensively under the best qualified guidance available in English lessons as well as practising it extensively with the help of understanding adults both in and outside school.

SUBJECT AND TEACHER

Suggested further reading

ABBS, P. (1976) *Root and Blossom: the Philosophy, Practice and Politics of English Teaching* Heinemann

ADAMS, A. (1970) *Team Teaching and the Teaching of English* Pergamon

ADAMS, A and PEARCE, J. (1974) *Every English Teacher* Oxford University Press

BAGNALL, N. (ed) (1973) *New Movements in the Teaching of English* Temple Smith

CRAIG, D. and HEINEMANN, M. (eds) (1976) *Experiments in English Teaching* Arnold

CREBER, J.W.P. (1966) *Sense and Sensitivity* London University Press

DIXON, J. (1975) *Growth Through English* Oxford University Press. Revised Edition

HOLBROOK, D. (1967) *The Exploring Word: Creative Disciplines in the Education of Teachers of English* Cambridge University Press

MARLAND, M. (ed) (1977) *Language Across the Curriculum* Heinemann

MATHIESON, M. (1975) *The Preachers of Culture* Allen and Unwin

OWENS, G. and MARLAND, M. (1970) *The Practice of English Teaching* Blackie

PALMER, D.J. (1965) *The Rise of English Studies* Oxford University Press

ROWE, A. (1975) *English Teaching and its Contribution to Secondary Education* Rupert Hart-Davis

SAUNDERS, M. (1976) *Developments in English Teaching* Open Books

SHAYER, D. (1972) *The Teaching of English in Schools 1900–1970* Routledge & Kegan Paul

SQUIRE, J.R. (1966) *A Common Purpose* National Council of Teachers of English (USA)

STRATTA, L., DIXON, J. and WILKINSON, A.M. (1973) *Patterns of Language: Explorations of the Teaching of English* Heinemann

WHITEHEAD, F. (1966) *The Disappearing Dais* Chatto and Windus

Language

7 What is language?

The spoken language comes first both historically and in importance in human intercourse. The point is underlined if we remember that the tongue is the most important and flexible organ in shaping the sounds of speech and that the word for tongue in many languages as well as our own is the synonym for language. Indeed the word 'language' comes via French from the Latin *lingua* meaning tongue. It is still necessary to stress the primacy of speech because, since the printed book became the first effective medium of mass communication in the fifteenth century, our culture and education have depended on literacy. Since the Renaissance education and literacy have become almost synonymous. Before that time and in many other civilizations a person might be highly educated but not literate.

Language, then, is a system or code of vocal (phonic) symbols which convey meaning between people who have learnt the system, people who belong to a 'language community'. It is therefore primarily a social convention linking people together though it is also personal in that no two members of a language community will use the language in precisely the same way.

Many languages have disappeared in the course of history but there are over two thousand still spoken in the world today, excluding dialects. Some of them have never been written down and many others have only been written quite recently in their long history. When we write or print a language we are using a system of visual (graphic) symbols standing for the vocal symbols of the spoken language and therefore twice removed from their message, whilst the Morse Code, for example, whose symbols composed of dots and dashes replace the visual symbols of the written language, is thrice removed. This is not to say, of course, that a person thoroughly conversant with these removed codes cannot take a short cut to the meaning without the intermediate stages of translation.

There are all manner of different sets of signs and their study is now called Semiotics but most of them are not languages in the full sense of the word. Some are internationally used like many of our road signs: others are only intelligible to people in a limited group or place: I know one school where the red, amber and green lights outside the headmaster's door mean, respectively 'Engaged', 'Out (try later)' and 'Knock and enter'. In addition, his secretary hangs her black umbrella on the hook inside the glass door of her adjacent office on days when 'The old man is in a bad mood'. This is a very simple system of agreed signs among a small group of people just as languages are very complex systems of agreed signs, vocal or visual, usually among much larger groups of people. Many animal species have quite elaborate systems of visual, vocal and other auditory signals, scent signals and touch signals for communicating such messages as 'Get off my patch', 'I'm looking for a mate', 'Danger!' and so on. Some of them can be taught to use and respond to signals which are not naturally instinctive to them. A dog may fetch its lead when it wants to go out or follow a shepherd's code of whistles. Chimpanzees have a natural code of signals and can learn others but if you bring up a baby chimp and a human infant together and treat them the same in every respect, the infant will rapidly acquire speech but the chimp will scarcely get beyond the gibbering stage. Man used to be defined as a tool-using animal and so he is but we now know that other creatures also use tools. He is much better described as language-using. The Sanskrit name for man, I have read, is translated as 'word-animal': but how does his language differ from animal and other codes of signals?

This is not a simple question and the difference is not solely one of complexity. In the first place language is acquired, not inherited. A young cuckoo reared in a hedge sparrow's or linnet's nest will develop vocally and in other respects into a normal cuckoo while a human infant will learn the speech and other behaviour patterns of the home in which it is brought up regardless of its parentage, race or colour. If it was reared by wild animals and there are a few recorded cases of this happening, it would be unable to speak. Secondly, the sound and visual signs of language (excepting some few onomatopoetic words and pictographic scripts) are arbitrary ones. We can see that even onomatopoetic words are still arbitrary conventional symbols if we compare, for example English 'purr' with French 'ronronner', or 'buzz' with German 'summen'. Many signs and sign systems are, by contrast, often in a stylised way more or less representational such as the road signs already mentioned. If one thinks of an Ordnance Survey map, some of the conventional signs are clearly representational (lighthouse, orchard), others partially so (crossed swords for a battlefield; an example of what might be called visual synecdoche); others are arbitrary (red dot and triangle for railway station and youth hostel), others again are abbreviated verbal signs (P for Post Office, P.H. for public house). Some signs like the striped barber's pole appear arbitrary having long since lost their original representational significance and the same process has affected many language signs. Roman numerals are more representational (and more cumbersome to use) than Arabic ones but both have different arbitrary sound signs attached to them in different languages (five, cinq, funf, cinco, pjat′, etc.).

The word 'symbol' refers properly to a sign devised or selected to represent something else. Symbols stand for and are synonyms for other signs whereas some signs are not symbols but only signals which carry messages and give immediate information. Thus a dog's growl, a factory hooter and a Belisha beacon are sign signals and 'one', '1' and the sound 'wun' are sign-symbols. So, finally, because language is a system of symbols, it enables man and only man to break the space/time barrier in communicating, it frees him from the here and now. He has a highly developed area of the brain, which is only rudimentary in other creatures, that enables him to symbolize. A dog can communicate present anger or joy but cannot say, 'I was angry with that cat yesterday' or, 'I will dig up that bone in the back garden tomorrow'. Language enables us to name, classify, evaluate, and compare; to order experience by considering the past and to plan the future. In a word it enables us to think.

The question, 'What is language?', though obviously complex, is well worth exploring with children. It is a great help if they are learning one or more languages other than English for there are some things about language which are difficult to grasp without a basis for comparison. At the very least children can try to invent a completely new language. In doing so they will quickly learn much that is basic about how language works. They will have to solve the problem of relating visual to vocal symbols. They will discover empirically the need for such categories of words as noun, verb, adjective, adverb and for 'operators' like prepositions, articles and conjunctions. They will soon discover the limitation of signs which are representational. They will be exploring the nature of symbolization and, indeed, of thinking.

It is an anomaly worth reflecting on that although English and foreign languages are studied in schools, language itself, its nature and functions, is almost totally ignored. Can we really assume that because we all use language we all understand what it is and how it works? It may be that some of the difficulties which language teachers encounter in their work arise from this strange omission and that there is here a real need and opportunity for innovation and integration by English and other language teachers.

8 What kind of language is English?

The first thing to say is that English is a foreign language so far as Britain is concerned. Welsh or Cymric was the language of what is now called England until the time of King Arthur. English is basically a Germanic dialect as we can see from the ready intelligibility of 'Der Winter ist kalt', 'Das Bier ist gut' and so on, though the Norman Conquest and later the 'ink-horn' vocabulary of post-Renaissance learning gave it some features of the Romance and Classical languages. The Frisian spoken in some parts of the Netherlands is the most nearly related to English of modern European languages. As an Indo-European language, however, English is related not only to Teutonic and Romance languages but to Celtic, Baltic and Slavonic languages, Greek, Armenian, Persian and some of the languages of the Indian sub-continent. Our position as an imperial and trading power has given and continues to give us a substantial vocabulary from many languages outside the Indo-European family as well.

'The English language', says Otto Jespersen, 'is a methodical, energetic, business-like and sober language, that does not care much for finery and elegance, but does care for logical consistency and is opposed to any attempt to narrow-in life by police regulations and strict rules of grammar or of lexicon. As the language is, so is the nation.' Elsewhere he says of English, 'it seems to me positively and expressly masculine'. With due respect to the memory of a great Danish philologist and Anglophile, these are highly subjective views.

The fact is that our feelings and associations get in the way of objective judgments about language, both other people's and varieties of our own, and most often they are chauvinistic feelings. Hence, to many Englishmen German sounds harsh and ugly, French effeminate or risqué and Spanish and Italian are redolent of vino, garlic, amorousness and sunshine. The more different a language from our own, the odder it sounds and looks and the easier it becomes to make fun of it. Thus all Chinese seem to have names like Wee Tin Po and eat flied lice.

Putting prejudice aside so far as is humanly possible, we have to say that in general, no language is intrinsically beautiful or ugly, or superior or inferior to any other language. For particular purposes one language may have advantages when compared with another. To take an often-quoted example, a relatively primitive people like the Eskimos have a vocabulary which enables them to talk about snow with a sophistication, accuracy and economy that is impossible in English and there is no justification for regarding their language as primitive, whatever the level of their material culture. Other languages understandably have no word for snow at all. The East African speaker of pidgin English, on the other hand, having no word for piano, has to say 'bokkis (box) you fight him, him call out'. He may, on the other hand, say 'Sorry, no can do' which is, perhaps, no less courteous and certainly more economical than 'I regret that I am unable to comply with your request'.

Had Jespersen said that English is a very hissy language (something that often strikes foreigners) this would have been objectively true, our two regular remaining inflexions, the possessive and the plural, both for historical reasons happening to be an s. Had he said that English is the only European language to have uninflected adjectives, or the highest percentage of monosyllabic words or the most varied assortment of foreign loan words, these facts would have been demonstrable. He might have said that English has about half a million words though 90 per cent of our use of English makes do with a mere ten thousand of them (and Basic English devised in the 1940s by Ogden and Richards gets by with eight hundred and fifty). More strikingly still, sixty-nine high-frequency words account for half of our use of English and ten of them account for a quarter, though English is not, of course, peculiar in this respect. He might have said that we have the most tiresome and unsystematically unphonetic spelling and, with French, an exceptional number of homophones (know/no, knew/new, knows/nose) and homonyms (fast – rapid, abstinence, firmly fixed). Anyone who has taught English as a foreign language knows that these features cause endless confusion.

If we consider grammar rather than vocabulary (structure rather than lexis as linguists tend now to say) we can sum up much that is characteristic of English even among closely related languages by saying that it is analytical (largely uninflected) rather than synthetic (inflected). In this respect it is nearer to Chinese than to German. Old English (Anglo-Saxon) was an inflected language like Latin and Greek and to some extent like modern Russian and German though it only had four cases of noun and adjective where its Indo-European ancestor had eight. Over the past nine hundred years we have lost most inflexions and, with a few exceptions, greatly simplified the rest. To put the same point another way, English has lost most of its formal grammar (accidence); instead of changing the forms of words to indicate relationships, number, gender, case, tense etc. English tends to use pronouns, prepositions, auxiliaries and word order so that the study of sentence structure (syntax) becomes relatively more important. Thus, where Latin has 'amaveram' and 'mensarum', English has 'I had loved' and 'of the tables'. Other related European languages have also become less inflected over the centuries but English has gone further than any other. This is the direction of change but it would be unscientific to call it progress. The Germanic languages all happen to have a tendency to place the stress towards the beginning of words so that the inflected endings tend to become less important. It has often been argued that the loss of flexibility in word order in an analytical language is more than compensated by the freedom with which one part of speech can be used as another. So we can say house boat/boat house, horse chestnut/chestnut horse, cake shop/shop cake and not need to make noun and adjective agree with each other either. Similarly adverbs and pronouns can be used as nouns and nouns readily formed into verbs so that in talking about gardening, for instance, weed, plant, seed, rake, hoe, shovel, water etc., could all be used as nouns or verbs (and some as adjectives, too). By combining our generous stock of prepositions with e.g. go, get, put, run etc., we have a great facility for generating new verbs.

At the level of phonology, a language may have as few as twenty or as many as seventy-five phonemes (the smallest contrastive unit of sound). The number of actual sounds our speech organs can make is, of course, almost limitless: the number our ears are trained to distinguish is very much smaller. German and French each have thirty-six phonemes and English with fourty-four is slightly above average and would need the same number of symbols, like the Initial Teaching Alphabet, for us to spell phonetically. That the names of four of our vowels are now pronounced as diphthongs (a [ei], i [ai], o [ou], u [iu]) is symptomatic of our problem. The great vowel shift which took place between the fifteenth and seventeenth centuries and after spelling had been more or less fixed by the printers has left us with the very unphonetic spelling alr^ady mentioned. Neither black sheep nor white ones really say 'Baa Baa', as anyone who has listened to them will know, but something much more like 'Bay, Bay'. It has been suggested that the abundance of diphthongs in English tends to make our pronunciation abnormally unstable. Our consonants have changed in sound much less since Anglo-Saxon times.

English, then, is a largely analytic Germanic language whose vocabulary has acquired layers of Scandinavian, French and Graeco-Roman words and whose orthography is unsystematically unphonetic. Thus to describe it may be the sober truth but is as bloodless as Bitzer's description of the horse as a graminivorous quadruped with forty teeth. We can all be forgiven for a degree of partiality for our own language, and English teachers, without being sissy, are hardly likely to be effective unless they have an abiding curiosity about it and a boundless enthusiasm for what it can be made to do.

9 What is correct English?

Many people who consider themselves educated, including many teachers in the past and, alas, not a few still today, suppose that 'good' or 'correct' English is governed by rules which are always applicable when the language is 'properly' spoken or written. This standard is often referred to as Queen's English or BBC English. On this view, regional variations of vocabulary, grammar or pronunciation as well as slang and colloquialism are always incorrect, inferior and to be deplored even if they are more excusable in some circumstances than others. There is no justification for this belief in a universally applicable standard of correctness, either in history or logic and it has done great harm. George Sampson noted its result in 1921: 'The majority of Englishmen are convinced that they can hope for nothing better in writing and speaking their own language than to avoid making asses of themselves'.

An alternative belief starts with the recognition that English, like all living languages, is used in very diverse circumstances for an immense range of human purposes: 'good' and therefore 'correct' English then becomes the register and style of language which suits the circumstances and fulfils the purpose most effectively. On this view, 'appropriateness' rather than 'correctness' becomes the useful yardstick. As Andrew Wilkinson has written, 'There is no point whatsoever in teaching children "Please take your foot out of my ear" for use in the playground where "gerroutovit" would be the appropriate word.' In the playground context 'gerroutovit' is better English. To argue that this is a preferable and more scientific view of language is *not* to suggest that 'anything goes' in children's writing and talking in school, or elsewhere. Children are perfectly familiar with the notion that all social behaviour is governed by conventions, manners and rules, and language behaviour is no exception. One doesn't lick one's knife when Granny comes to tea or say out loud in the street 'look at that fat woman in the funny hat' or end a letter to a prospective employer 'Cheerio for now'. We are indulgent about the *faux pas* of little children and help them without censoriousness to become more socially aware in the process of growing up and to judge with ever increasing nicety what is the appropriate kind of language to use in different situations. And this need not exclude language which is calculated to shock or offend in some circumstances; a neutered, insipid, safe language is not the aim but one that is genuinely expressive of the user's thoughts and feelings while at the same time restrained, of course, by consideration for others.

Standard English (SE) is one dialect among many and Received Pronunciation (RP) with which it is associated is one accent among many. The three greatest literary masterpieces of the fourteenth century: *The Canterbury Tales*, *Piers Plowman* and *Sir Gawain and the Green Knight* were written respectively in the South-East, the South-West Midlands and the North-West. They were written at more or less the same time, in varieties of English very different from each other to the point in parts of being mutually unintelligible. Today Chaucer's Tales are very much easier to read because they are closer to modern Standard English than the other two great poems. Why? The answer is that the regional dialect in which he wrote was from that part of the country which included London, with the court and seat of government, and the two ancient universities at Oxford and Cambridge. It is not surprising, then, that it tended to become the official version of the language and that of most educated people.

When, in the middle of the next century, Caxton set up his printing press in London, he was very conscious of the problem that the 'comyn englysshe that is spoken in one shyre varyeth from another'. He tells the story of a merchant away from home who called at a house and asked for 'egges'; the housewife thought he was speaking French for she called them 'eyren' and could not understand him. 'Loo what sholde a mane in thyse dayes now wryte', exclaims Caxton, 'certaynly it is harde to playse every man by cause of dyversite and chaunge of language'. His English is not difficult for us to read after five hundred years because the solution to his problem was inevitable. He printed his books and translated foreign works into the dialect of the London area and that dialect which has become Standard English subsequently became the one most closely associated with the printed word. For this reason it has been the variety of English most universally understood though, today, an American accent is the most familiar way of pronouncing it around the world.

Clearly, then, Standard English and Received Pronunciation have acquired great importance and prestige but it is essential to remember that other dialects and accents are equally ancient and authentic varieties of English. They are not debased or ugly or slovenly or incorrect. The English are notoriously quick to pass judgment on varieties of their language so that Shaw says, in the Preface to Pygmalion, 'it is impossible for an Englishman to open his mouth without making some other Englishman despise him'. When pejorative judgments are made about varieties of non-standard English, questions of dialect vocabulary, dialect grammar and accent are often confused and so it is, perhaps, necessary to say a brief word about each though they are, of course, interrelated aspects of speech.

To take vocabulary first, a regional dialect speaker will use a number of non-standard words which would only be found in a dialect dictionary. Children, in my experience, do not often use dialect words in lessons unless encouraged to do so. The whole question of why there are different varieties of English can be a fascinating one to explore with them and with a little guidance they can be involved in field work of scholarly importance. My left-handed son, when he went to school in the Staffordshire Potteries was called a 'keggy-onded lommock' (a lommock is a large lump or a clumsy fellow). This was playground rather than classroom language. In Yorkshire he might have been called a 'cuddy-wifter', in Durham a 'gallocker', in the South-West 'cam-anded' or 'skivvy-anded' and so on. The Dialect Survey of Professors Orton and Dieth recorded more than a dozen other expressions for left-handed. Similarly my son had to learn that you 'flirt' rather than throw a ball, that 'cuthering' is whispering, to 'sneap' is to snub or vex someone and a hill is almost always called a bank. Often words which have survived in only a limited area go back to Anglo-Saxon or Old Norse while their Standard English equivalents may be much more recent importations into the language. People often regard regional dialect words in a rather patronising way as quaint and curious and worthy of preservation, like timber-framed buildings or the stocks on the village green, and the mass media are blamed for disappearing dialects.

Dialect grammar is, by contrast, seldom accorded such tolerance. Some of my son's school mates would say, for example, 'It were 'im as towd us to gi' 'im us biuks', where the words all belong to Standard English but the grammar and pronunciation do not. This is much more likely to be called 'wrong' or 'bad' or even 'shocking' English and this is odd for two reasons. Firstly, non-standard grammar is much less likely to be unintelligible than non-standard vocabulary: in what circumstances would 'Him and me done it, Miss' fail to communicate as readily as 'He and I did it'? Secondly, though regional speech may retain earlier forms like 'housen' for 'houses', it is often Standard English grammar which is old-fashioned and clumsy and the regional variation which is economical and logical. For example, we do not need an inflected verb 'to be' and the West-country man who says 'I be, you be, he be, we be, you be, they be' is only carrying to its logical conclusion the process which has already overtaken most of our verbs and to this extent he is speaking better grammar than that of Standard English. Similarly 'you was' which was correct until the late eighteenth century and comes from the earlier 'thou wast' retains the distinction between singular and plural which we lose when we use 'you were' for both.

As to pronunciation, regional accents are *different* from Received Pronunciation, particularly in their vowel sounds but only snobbish ignorance would call them ugly, uncouth or slovenly. Received Pronunciation has no monopoly of beautiful sounds. Some of my students, who come from all over the country, catch the bus [ʌ] to Newcastle [a] with southern vowels; others catch the boos [u] to Newcastle [æ] with northern vowels. Both groups are equally likely to slur their speech sounds through lazy articulation, to the point where they become difficult to follow. The miner's son from Barnsley who sounds the g in words like singer and singing is being less lazy than the ex-public school boy from Broadstairs who doesn't. Clear intelligible speech depends far more on the speaker's vigorous articulation than on the broadness of his accent and this holds good whether we are talking about the educated or uneducated, the upper crust or the working class, countrymen or townsfolk, northerners or southerners, native English speakers or foreigners.

In conclusion, then, 'correctness' and 'incorrectness' are not very useful concepts and best avoided in discussing questions concerning our use of our own language. Good English is English that is most effective in promoting understanding between speaker and listener, writer and reader and will be as various as the situations in which people seek to understand each other and express themselves. I shall have something to say about correctness of spelling and punctuation in connection with creative writing in a later chapter.

10 Should children be taught standard English?

The kind of language children grow up to use at home and in the playground is their own business rather than the school's, although, like other aspects of out-of-school activity it obviously impinges on the school's work. We have already said that however different it is from Standard English and Received Pronunciation it is neither incorrect nor debased *per se* in its power of effective communication. As Halliday, McIntosh and Strevens say, 'A speaker who is made ashamed of his own language habits suffers a basic injury as a human being: to make anyone, especially a child, feel so ashamed is as indefensible as to make him feel ashamed of the colour of his skin'. Do all English teachers have a clear conscience in this respect?

We have also said that Standard English and Received Pronunciation have certain rather obvious advantages which we want children to enjoy as far as possible. Standard English is the normal written form of the language and children need to become effectively literate to cope with our society. They are also the most widely intelligible forms of the spoken language and we want to give children the opportunity to be effective communicators outside the limits of their immediate geographical and social environment, as well as within it. A Geordie and a Devonshire man may speak varieties of English at home which would be almost unintelligible to each other but both will readily understand Standard English particularly in an age of mass communications. Evidence suggests that when they meet they will quite naturally and without conscious effort tend to modify their regional speech in the direction of Standard English and Received Pronunciation, so that most non-Standard dialect speakers are today already to some extent bilingual in their own language.

The natural informal and familiar chatter of home and playground is entirely appropriate in its place. Communication in school is equally naturally rather more formal. The teacher may not be a native of the district and some of the children may have roots in other parts of the country or abroad. Even if they were all born within a stone's throw of the school, the school is not only concerned with the immediate environment of the children. It is in business to open up wider horizons of space and time, even if it sensibly often works outwards from what is already familiar at first hand.

The sensible answer to the question should children be taught Standard English is this. They should be helped to expand the range of situations they can handle with increasing self -confidence and without loss of identity. This means that we will help and encourage them *when appropriate*, to modify their language in the direction of Standard English and Received Pronunciation, but with the important proviso that, as J.L.M. Trim says, 'there should be no contempt for the speech of the home and of playmates, no imposition of formal speech as a higher, purer, better type, irrespective of context'. Their own natural language, however broadly regional, is not inferior to Standard English in flexibility or expressive potential. Indeed, people are always likely to express themselves most forcefully in the form of language that is most natural to them and should usually be encouraged to do so – in their creative work, for instance. Children, as children, will rarely if ever have occasion to use the most formal kinds of written or spoken communication though they will meet them, by and by, in their reading and in their contacts with the formal transactions of the adult world. There is good reason to think that the content of a scientific treatise, say, or a parliamentary speech could be conveyed in some non-standard variety of English perfectly adequately. It would, however, be distractingly unconventional to convey it in that way and, as we have stressed, to learn a language is to learn a complex social convention.

There are sensitive and, in a wide sense, political issues raised here. To teach conventions in the old way as unquestionably correct is to perpetuate, albeit unintentionally a class-divided society. To teach linguistic facts in isolation from questions of social attitudes could be construed as *using* children in the hope of changing that society. Facts about a language cannot be separated from facts about the society that uses it. It is a fact of linguistics as well as of sociology that a regional accent and, more particularly, non-standard grammar in speech or writing may limit job opportunities and social acceptability generally because they are still associated by many people with low social status and lack of education or intelligence or sophistication, however unjustifiable such attitudes may be. It would be doing children a disservice to conceal this from them.

The modified bilingual approach which I have suggested is a compromise: it would not be acceptable to all linguists or sociologists. It does, however, represent a great advance on older notions of 'correctness' while taking account of the undoubted facts of prejudice and convention in our society.

11 What are the basic skills and should we be anxious about standards?

I have suggested that English is centrally concerned with skills rather than knowledge – skills in using language. At a sophisticated level these skills may be concerned with nice judgments in choosing and arranging language in composition and with perception, interpretation and discrimination in reading literature which should be inseparable from responses and judgments in life generally. For the moment, however, we are concerned with skills at a more basic level.

With the introduction of compulsory elementary education for all at the end of last century, the basic skills of education were thought of as the three Rs and English was concerned with two of them, reading and writing. After the Second World War the old Three Rs notion of the basic skills was clearly no longer adequate. There was a brief period in education of infatuation with audio-visual equipment and it was even argued that the first need of future generations would be 'mediacy' or 'all-media literacy'. The Jeremiahs of doom and decadence lamented that the Three Rs had been replaced by the Three Ls (Look, Listen and Laze), that teachers were happily projecting pictures and playing tapes while children slumbered in the dark fug of their illiteracy. A measure of sanity quickly returned but clearly we could not simply go back. The notion of the Three Rs as the basic skills needed revising for the second half of the twentieth century.

In an age of science and technology, computers and automation, mathematics had become relatively more important than ever before. The 'Rithmetic of the old formulation was clearly inadequate for those skills in the language of number now needed by everybody and so the word 'numeracy' was coined in the 1950s, given wide currency by the Crowther Report of 1959 and much exploited in the 'Two Cultures' debate initiated by Lord Snow. By the mid-1960s the word had found a place in the Penguin Dictionary.

Similarly with Reading and 'Riting; they covered only two of the language skills and the skills of the spoken word, speaking (or oral composition) and listening (or aural comprehension) could no longer be neglected in an age of mass communication. When, after the war, television and the tape recorder were added to the telephone, gramophone, radio and sound-film we had a formidable array of means for transmitting and recording language which did not depend essentially on reading and writing at all. And so the useful word 'oracy' was coined for those skills of the spoken word which we are only now beginning to study and learn how to teach and test. It will find its way into dictionaries soon if it has not already done so.

Literacy, of course, is still indispensable and likely to remain so into the forseeable future. Today it must include the reference skills which are sometimes referred to as the Fourth R if it is to remain a relevant concept. But literacy can never again assume the unique importance it had during the four hundred years after Gutenberg invented movable lead type when the printed word was the only mass medium of communication. Thus, in the past few years, educationalists have begun to talk about the basic skills as the NOL skills. Certainly an educated person today needs to be Numerate, Orate and Literate but to talk about the NOL skills is, I believe, to replace one inadequate trinity with another. The revolution in communications has surely been a *visual* as well as an oral and aural one; indisputably we are learning more from pictures and getting more of our recreation and leisure from looking at them. This suggests that there must be skills of looking every bit as important and potentially corrigible as the skills of number, speech and writing, which as yet we scarcely understand. The phrase 'visual literacy' has been current in the Art College world for some time but these skills of looking must be too basic to be left entirely to the art educator just as oracy and literature are too basic to be entirely the responsibility of English teachers. In 1965 I suggested that we need another neologism, perhaps 'videacy' for these skills of looking. More recently, Professor W.G.V. Balchin, a geographer, has proposed 'graphicacy'. Maybe someone else will come up with a happier alternative and it, too, will find its way into the dictionary in time.

However this may be, English teachers are centrally concerned with promoting literacy and oracy. Unfortunately much confusion surrounds the idea of literacy, and the idea of oracy is likely to be similarly bedevilled when it is equally commonly used in debates about education and standards.

With the word 'literacy' the problem is that it does not indicate a fixed standard. A person who is illiterate in the strict sense is unable to read or write at all. Figures of literacy and illiteracy for other countries and for past periods of our own history are usually based on the number of people who had to make their mark because they couldn't sign their name in a marriage register or other similar document. A person who *can* read or write, however, may be more or less literate. When UNESCO reports that 70 per cent of the population of India is illiterate and when a university vice-chancellor complains about the illiteracy of the present generation of undergraduates the word is clearly being used in two different senses. In the latter, seemingly anyone can be called illiterate who is less literate than someone else thinks he should be. All talk about literacy and all comparative statistics, therefore, need to be approached with extreme caution: we always need to ask what is meant by literacy, by what criteria it is being measured and to what section of a population the figures apply. When the adult literacy campaign was launched in 1975 we were constantly told that there were two million adult illiterates in this country but not even the educational press revealed or even appeared to be concerned to know how this figure was arrived at.

Concern about standards of literacy is a persistent social anxiety and has been for generations past. It is generally supposed that standards have fallen and continue to fall. In the 1930s the depression was blamed, in the 1940s the war, in the 1950s television, in the 1960s play-way methods in primary schools and today comprehensive reorganization comes in for a good deal of stick: indeed, anything we fear or dislike may be made into a scapegoat. The standard people have in mind is generally some notion of adequate or functional literacy, some recollection of how things used to be, without troubling to check whether like is being compared with like. Functional literacy, however, is a relative standard culturally determined.

As UNESCO put it, 'A person is functionally literate when he has acquired the knowledge and skills of reading and writing which enable him to engage effectively in all those activities in which literacy is normally assumed in his culture or group'. A person might be functionally literate in an undeveloped country but quite inadequately literate to cope in an industrialized society like our own. In 1975 the Bullock committee scrutinized all the available evidence about standards of literacy in this country and concluded that none of it pointed unambiguously to any absolute decline in the literacy of school leavers. On the contrary, there had been a steady rise in standards since the war which had tended to level out in the decade up to 1970. This does not, of course, mean that there are no grounds for anxiety. It is certainly true that a standard which can be regarded as functionally adequate today is a more exacting one than ever before and the number of jobs in our society for which a high level of literacy is not a prerequisite has fallen dramatically. To take a simple example, a young farm worker who was crudely literate but quite able to do his job just after the war might well be a liability on a farm today with complicated machinery, pesticides, fertilizers and record-keeping. Quite apart from work, even the most literate of us must sometimes find our skills taxed to the limit by some of the forms, regulations and conditions which any citizen may be required to complete or comply with. The least literate may often be those who have the greatest claims on the social services but are least able to cope with the bureaucracy that administers them. There is good reason to believe that raising the school leaving age twice since the war and other educational reforms have not enabled us to keep pace with the increasing demands made on people's basic skills. As the Bullock Report says, 'It is obvious that as our society becomes more complex and makes higher demands in awareness and understanding of its members the criteria of literacy will rise'. Thinking of such literature as tax return guides, claims for social security benefits and the Highway Code they say, 'the lowest grade of difficulty at which complex subject matter can be written approximates to a reading age of about fifteen'. Very often such material, as we all know to our cost, is not expertly simplified but couched in dauntingly quasi-legal language. Seen in this light, a figure of two million adult illiterates must be an underestimate and there is no doubt that we have a problem of functional literacy which will not be solved by English teachers alone or even by schools with a concerted language policy.

In our anxiety about literacy as a means to the convenient running of a complex society, we should not confuse quantity of literacy with quality. The value of skills in a personal, educational sense depends on how they are used. English teachers in particular will want to ask constantly whether the things written or read are, convenience apart, worth writing or reading. At a time when most reformers naively supposed that literacy would be instrumental in saving the souls of the masses by making the Scriptures available to them, William Cobbett showed a healthy scepticism when he said, 'I must hear a great deal more than I have heard, to convince me that teaching children to read tends so much to their happiness, independence and manliness'. The greater the social pressures for training children in utilitarian skills, the more educators with wider liberal ideals need to be on their guard.

12 What ought we to teach children about their own language?

This question – notice the 'ought' – is a value question: people's judgments about it will inevitably differ, though some judgments may be shown to be well- or ill-founded in the light of research evidence. It is also, like so many curriculum questions, one which cannot be usefully answered without specifying the age and ability of the children one has in mind. In offering a brief personal answer to it I shall, in the main, be summarizing the suggestions and implications of earlier sections.

If we start with the older and abler pupil, it is an anomaly that at A level the study of English should be so exclusively literary. In 1964, Randolf Quirk argued in an appendix to the eighth report on the Secondary Schools Examinations Council for an alternative A level paper in Modern English Language and provided a specimen syllabus and question paper. That his initiative has led to few, if any positive developments, probably reflects the lack of teachers in schools with the linguistic training to teach pupils at this level about the variety, nature, grammatical and lexical resources and transmission systems of present day English. It could certainly be an interesting and properly challenging analytical discipline. If the teachers were there and the subject well taught it would be reasonable to expect a significant proportion of candidates to choose to do one language and two literature papers instead of three literary ones. Sixth forms, however, are a special case: pupils choose their subjects and options within them and we are no nearer answering our question for the majority of pupils.

It used to be argued that for all pupils some knowledge of the structure of English and some formal study of the language was obviously necessary if they were to learn to write and speak effectively and correctly, to be 'functionally literate' in fact. We have already queried the usefulness of this notion of correctness. In a Ministry of Education publication (Pamphlet

No. 26, 1954) called *Language: Some Suggestions for Teachers of English and Others* the anonymous author refers to the 'ancient and wearisome controversy about grammar' as 'no more than shadow boxing'. He continues, 'It is only reasonable to suppose that a knowledge of the structure of sentences is useful at a certain stage [he doesn't say when] in learning to write. To this most experienced teachers of English would add an acquaintance with the parts of speech and their function. Much of this necessary grammatical groundwork involves drill.' After saying that in grammar schools one period a week for three years should suffice for this drill but that more time might be needed with less able children, he concludes, 'a systematic study of grammar by older and abler pupils is another matter altogether'. This is the only paragraph devoted to grammar in a book of one hundred and sixty-nine pages and it is manifestly unhelpful and evasive.

The 'ancient and wearisome controversy' was often confused by terminology: teachers argued whether or not 'formal grammar' should be taught to children. It may be as well, as an aside, to try and clear up that confusion. Formal grammar is concerned with the changing forms of words or accidence. English, as we have seen, has relatively very little surviving formal grammar. Admittedly there was a time when English accidence was taught exactly on the Latin pattern but, after the mid-1920s, the controversy was about whether functional grammar, that is to say the structure of sentences or syntax, should be taught *formally* and systematically, *informally* and piecemeal as the need arose in the hope that it would help children to avoid supposed mistakes, or not at all.

In fact by 1954 when the Ministry's pamphlet was published the 'wearisome' argument should have been settled by research once and for all and, if the author was right about 'most teachers' they were hopelessly out of touch with the available evidence. As early as 1903 research in America by J.M. Rice strongly suggested that learning grammar had no beneficial effect on children's written work and numerous studies in the next half-century confirmed this suspicion beyond all doubt. Catherine Catherwood in 1932 and M.C. Benfer in 1935 both found a poor correlation between knowledge of grammar and the ability to correct sentences containing grammatical 'mistakes'. In 1947 W.J. Macaulay showed that it was pointless to teach even such basic grammatical concepts as the parts of speech before the age of fourteen because most children were not intellectually ready to grasp them. Other researches had suggested that much grammar teaching was not merely nugatory but actually hampered children's ability to express themselves effectively and might adversely affect their attitude to English as a whole. It is a shocking story of a failure of communications and yet, in view of the official pronouncements of the Ministry's pamphlet, it is hardly surprising that grammar continued to feature in examination syllabuses for many years and still does so in not a few course-books published for younger secondary and even for primary school classes.

Another reason sometimes advanced for teaching English grammar was that it must be an indispensable prerequisite for learning other languages, whether ancient and dead, or modern and living. This view seems to be equally ill-founded. S.L. Pressey showed in 1934 that a knowledge of English grammar is helpful in learning other languages only if they are approached through grammatical categories but this approach to language is now discredited and, if Macaulay's conclusions about a grammar-readiness age are right, this comes after most children have started to study other languages. There is no evidence that a knowledge of grammar is helpful to direct method learning. Even if a formal grammatical approach to language learning is adopted, it is not clear that the *English* teacher should teach the necessary minimum of grammar. For reasons previously discussed, a knowledge of English grammar might be more confusing than helpful in learning more highly inflected languages like German, Russian, Latin and Greek. In the same way, the study of Anglo-Saxon, a highly inflected language, is of doubtful relevance to students of English at University level except, of course, as the means of access to Old English literature.

In an earlier section I suggested that there might be a good case for introducing children to the questions, what is language and how does it work and the time for such a project might be just before they start learning a language or languages other than English. It seems to me that this ought to be a team-teaching exercise which should explore these fascinating questions for their own sake first, but it could have the very real incidental advantage of showing children some of the differences and similarities between English and the other languages they are going to study and in avoiding the confusion that often arises when different language teachers use different terminology for the same grammatical forms and functions.

To return to our initial question, what ought we to teach children about their language, we can at least say at this stage that we ought not to teach grammar in the traditional way. The arguments for doing so will not stand up to examination. Instead, we could argue that since children have already learnt to use all the basic structures of English before they even come to school, it is pointless to teach them grammar. They also come to school with a sizeable vocabulary (at least 2000 words at the age of five and twice as many two years later) and they will add to this stock progressively with experience and in response to the need to express and communicate. It would be pointless and artificial to teach vocabulary in isolation from that need. Our language at any stage is an integral part of our personality and its growth and refinement indissolubly linked with personal mental development. It is the same with our bodies in respect of personal physical development. We do not, initially at least, teach children in any detail how their bodies work, anatomy, physiology, neurology and so on; rather we teach them through exercise to *use* their bodies efficiently. By analogy we should teach them to exercise and use their language and, in performance, knowledge of accidence and syntax is as irrelevant as knowledge of anatomy and physiology. At an appropriate stage of development we will teach them some human biology and something about how language works and a few of them may even want to specialize in pursuing these subjects to an advanced level.

Having said all this are we, in effect, saying that children should be taught nothing about their language until the age of fourteen or later? Not necessarily so. We try to make life interesting for children by opening their eyes to many aspects of their environment: we teach them about natural history and the weather, about buildings and scenery, about local agriculture and industry and government. I had a colleague once who was passionately interested in meteorology; the most casual remark about the weather was likely to elicit from him a torrent of facts and figures about temperature and precipitation, cyclones and fronts. Happy man – he could, like any enthusiast, be a bore but never bored because there was always weather around in which to take an interest. Now language, like weather, is all around us all the time. A Professor Higgins should never be bored except, perhaps, in solitude. The English language with all its varieties and functions, both spoken and written, is indubitably a part of our environment, which may too easily pass unnoticed because it is taken for granted, but with appropriate knowledge, children's eyes and ears can be opened. The children's own names, local place names and many of the words that crop up in classroom talking and reading will often have fascinating histories as well as shapes, sounds and meanings. (The word 'fascinating' itself has a fascinating history connected originally with witchcraft and the evil eye.) Choice scraps of information about etymology together with observing the varieties of accent and dialect may be the best ways of arousing children's interest in and curiousity about their language. Arousing such curiosity and interest should be a continuous preoccupation of all English teachers. If they are successful in this, it will help enormously in their other constant aims: building up children's self-confidence and adventurousness in self-expression and encouraging their exploration of the world of books.

LANGUAGE

Suggested further reading

BANTOCK, G.H. (1966) *The Implications of Literacy* University of Leicester Press

BARNES, D. et al. (1971) *Language, the Learner and the School* Penguin

BRITTON, J. (1970) *Language and Learning* Penguin

CREBER, J.W.P. (1972) *Lost for Words* Penguin

DARBYSHIRE, A.E. (1967) *A Description of English* Arnold

DAVIES, H.S. (1961) *Grammar Without Tears* Bodley Head

DOUGHTY, A. and P. (1974) *Language and Community* Arnold

DOUGHTY, P. (1972) *Exploring Language* Arnold

FLOWER, F.D. (1966) *Language and Education* Longman
HALLIDAY, F.E. (1975) *The Excellency of the English Tongue* Gollancz
HALLIDAY, M.A.K., McINTOSH, A. and STREVENS, P. (1964) *The Linguistic Sciences and Language Teaching* Longman
LAWTON, D. (1968) *Social Class, Language and Education* Routledge & Kegan Paul
POTTER, S. (1966) *Language in the Modern World* Penguin (Revised Edition)
QUIRK, R. (1962) *The Use of English* Longman
STUBBS, M. (1976) *Language, Schools and Classrooms* Methuen
THORNTON, G. (1974) *Language, Experience and School* Arnold
THORNTON, G. and DOUGHTY, P. (1973) *Language Study, the Teacher and the Learner* Arnold
TRUDGILL, P. (1975) *Accent, Dialect and the School* Arnold
WILKINSON, A.M. (1971) *The Foundations of English* Oxford University Press
WILKINSON, A.M. (1975) *Language and Education* Oxford University Press
WILKINSON, A.M. (1965) *Spoken English* Educational Review Occasional Publications No. 2 University of Birmingham
Language in Education (1972) Open University/Routledge

Literature

13 What is literature?

Of the 2,800-odd living languages today, only about fifty have produced a literature of any size or significance. The majority of the world's population speaks a language in which a literature does exist but many of them are illiterate and the reading of it may be confined to a small élite class. Literature, unlike the other arts, has no medium distinctly its own: it has to use the same language which is used by everybody all the time for their everyday expression and social communication.

The word 'literature' is clearly used in at least two distinct senses. In the broader sense (from Latin *litera*) the word means simply whatever is written or printed and is used purely descriptively. Thus, we can talk about the literature on a topic, the sex-life of snails, say, or Chinese glazes of the Sung Dynasty. In the narrower sense the word is used evaluatively meaning, to quote Webster's dictionary 'writings having excellence of form or expression and expressing ideas of permanent or universal interest'. It is a pity, perhaps, that the word 'illiterature' has become obsolete or that Colet's word 'blotterature' never caught on: both were once used of works which aspired to be literature in this narrower sense but were deemed not to merit serious consideration. It is also a convenience (though strictly a nonsense) to call 'oral literature' those legends, sagas, folk tales, ballads and rhymes which existed in pre-literate societies as part of an oral tradition, often for many centuries before they came to be written down.

When the word is used in talk about teaching English at any level, it is likely to be the narrower, qualitative sense that is intended and the dictionary definition raises more questions than it answers. To start with, many famous books expressing important ideas are not necessarily distinguished by excellence of form or expression. 'Great Books' may have intellectual distinction or aesthetic merit but not necessarily both. The literature that is peculiarly the province of English scholars and teachers is therefore often further qualified (misleadingly, as we shall see) as 'imaginative literature' or *belles-lettres* to distinguish it from great works of history, theology, philosophy, science or whatever. More importantly, the question arises, How do we know that a piece of writing, poem, play or novel has the quality to be called 'literature' in the narrower sense or is indeed truly 'imaginative literature'? This is obviously a difficult question but, as with other difficult questions we have touched upon, I am convinced it will be raised explicitly or implicitly by the pupils of any successful English teacher and he must be ready to explore it with them at an appropriate level.

To ask whether a piece of writing is 'literature' is to ask whether it is 'good'. To answer that this is a question of purely personal preference and that there is no disputing about matters of taste is an argument-stopper frequently used by unsophisticated people generally. If we find children using it, we have probably unwittingly been asking them to make literary judgments before they are old enough to do so, as we will discuss later. The answer does contain an element of truth for there must be a personal, subjective element in all value judgments but it is false in suggesting that this is *all* they contain: a crude subjectivism is unsatisfactory for a number of reasons. In the first place people *do* dispute about questions of value in the arts as in morality and believe that something other than their own preferences is at stake. If it were true that 'nothing is either good or bad but thinking makes it so', then to dispute about aesthetic or moral questions would be as silly as for one man to say, 'I like curry', and another to retort, 'No, you're quite wrong. I can't stand the stuff.' The trouble doubtless began when the word 'taste' was extended from simple gustatory preferences to our perceptions of works of art where we feel that our preferences can and should be supported by persuasive reasons and objective evidence. The second objection is that there is a great deal of writing and little of it is likely to be literature of high quality. If we could only be guided by our own judgment, life would be too short ever to find the grains of wheat that satisfied our appetite in the great chaff heap. We need assurances of value from guides we can respect. Thirdly, the similarities between human beings in what causes them pleasure and pain, delight or disgust, are at least as conspicuous as the differences. As Hume says in his famous essay 'Of the Standard of Taste', 'The same Homer, who pleased at Athens and Rome two thousand years ago, is still admired at Paris and at London. All the changes of climate, government, religion and language have not been able to obscure his glory. Authority or prejudice may give a temporary vogue to a bad poet or orator; but his reputation will never be durable or general.'

Now it could be objected that Homer is a very special case and that probably most of the citizens of the four cities Hume mentions never cared a fig for Homer anyway. However, Hume has surely suggested the most obvious criterion for deciding what is literature in the qualitative sense – its permanence or durability. We may never have got around to reading Sophocles or Dante, Goethe or Tolstoy, or even Spenser and Milton but the fact that these writers and indeed lesser ones have had durable reputations offers us the best guarantee available that it would be worth our while to do so. But Hume was too sensible (about aesthetic matters, anyway, which he cared about passionately) to suppose that the merits of Homer or any other artist were to be settled by holding a census or counting votes. Not all men were equally well qualified by learning or experience to make value judgments about literature or to be called critics. 'Strong sense, united to delicate sentiment, improved by practice, perfected by comparison, and cleared of all prejudice, can alone entitle critics to this valuable character; and the joint verdict of such, wherever they are to be found, is the true standard of taste and of beauty.' There really was, he believed, such a consensus among those best qualified to judge.

Plainly there are difficulties in holding this view: eminent critics do sometimes disagree and who is to say whether a man has delicate sentiments or could ever clear his mind of all prejudice? Still, an imperfect standard cautiously applied is preferable to no standard at all and less narrow than purely personal preference. There is the real danger too, particularly when literature becomes the subject of formal study and examinations that value judgments will be hypocritically adopted at second hand from authority. This danger is avoided if the criterion of permanence is applied at a personal as well as an historical level. A work of literary merit will pre-eminently be one which is not exhausted at first reading but provides an increasingly rewarding experience the more often it is returned to. To quote Hume's essay once more, 'before we can give judgment on any work of importance, it will even be requisite that that very individual performance be more than once perused by us, and be surveyed in different lights with attention and deliberation. There is a flutter or hurry of thought which attends the first perusal of any piece, and which confounds the genuine sentiment of beauty.' The reviewer of recently published books cannot apply the criterion of permanence in either the historical or the personal sense and this is what distinguishes his task from criticism even if he is an eminent critic. Many books have been universally condemned when they first appeared and only subsequently recognized as masterpieces. All this has most important implications for teaching literature which we will come to later.

Much else can be and has been said to distinguish imaginative literature from literature in the wider sense: it will not be merely informative; what is said in paraphrasable terms may be less significant than how it is said: in other words the medium and its manipulation may be more important than, and is certainly inseparable from, the message. Often, but not always it deals with a fictional, invented world rather than the factual real one. Again, Newman said that 'Literature stands related to man as science stands to nature' and Professor W.R. Niblett once wrote that 'Literature brings to consciousness what is involved in being human'. Both are suggesting that, unlike scientific writing, literature deals with human experience in all its complexity, not merely what men have thought about the external world but also what they have felt, what they have thought about what they have felt and what they have felt about what they have thought. And so, if space were unlimited, we could go on collecting apophthegms and generalizations all true and helpful up to a point.

The important thing to say in conclusion is that most of the world's great literature was written by and for highly sophisticated and literate *adults* long since dead. Most of it by definition, therefore, will be inappropriate reading matter for most of today's youngsters most of the time. There is, of course, no sudden transition from unsophisticated adolescence to sophisticated adulthood and older and abler pupils need a challenge. Some undoubted masterpieces can be read at different levels with enjoyment: *The Ancient Mariner* might be a case in point and Shakespeare's plays delighted illiterate groundlings as well as courtiers and scholars. However, nothing in traditional English teaching has done greater harm than forcing on young people a premature acquaintance with great works of adult literature in the mistaken belief that they should not leave school without some contact with this part of 'our cultural heritage'. Of course we want to do all we can to share our own delight in literature; no purpose could be more admirable; but this will mean, in practice, building in our pupils as a foundation the habit of reading appropriate good books with enjoyment and gradually increasing powers of perception and discrimination so that, as adults, great works of adult literature may be accessible to them. Not many of these good books initially will be great literature or likely to attract the attention of academic literary critics.

The practical question for teachers then, who have to select what to make available to children is two-fold. First, what works of indubitable literary merit – or what parts of them – can be read and enjoyed by or with youngsters at what ages and stages? This is an empirical question about which there is a great deal of accumulated experience for guidance. Secondly, how does one choose among the mass of material written either for adults or specifically for youngsters the more worthwhile books to put in their way? This is a value question not essentially different, I believe, from the fundamental problems of literary evaluation. Writing about the plethora of narrative publications for children and adolescents, the authors of the Schools Council Working Paper *Children's Reading Interests* (1975) detect 'two fairly distinct groups – on the one hand those whose production has been essentially a commercial operation, a matter of catering for a market; and on the other hand those in which the involvement of the writer with his subject-matter and his audience has been such as to generate a texture of imaginative experience which rises above the merely routine and derivative'. In deciding on the quality of a book, the question they asked themselves was, 'Is this book one that we can imagine a responsible teacher justly recommending to pupils at a certain stage of development on the ground that they are likely to take from it some imaginative experience valuable to them at their own level, over and above the mere practice of reading skills?' This is essentially the same question teachers and school librarians must ask themselves. In answering it they will be guided by their understanding of child psychology and the accumulated experience of enlightened and successful teachers as well as by the two-fold criterion of permanence. That a children's book has stood the test of time will be some guide to quality, but the fact that all books become dated in some respect may be a particularly relevant consideration since children do not have the historical sense to make allowances and adjustments. Whether the book can retain the teacher's own respect and interest after first reading will be even more crucial in deciding whether it is worth children spending school time on it. C.S. Lewis has bluntly but wisely said, 'A book which is only liked by children is a bad children's book'.

The answer to the question, What is literature, in a school context, then, will be somewhat different from that in a university or adult context. It will include some indubitable great works, some adult books of quality, particularly recent ones and some children's books. The criteria of selection will be somewhat different too, in taking into account the age and ability of the children and other local and individual circumstances but not necessarily less rigorously applied. The teacher will be guided partly by his own and other teachers' experience, by reviewers and critics, by his knowledge of his pupils and also by his own preferences. It may be possible to recommend with confidence but not, perhaps, to teach with conviction, books whose qualities he can recognize but does not respond to in a strong and personal way. His task is dauntingly complex. He must start from where his pupils already are if he is to influence positively their reading tastes and habits. There are better and worse examples within all the categories of reading matter that may already be popular: science fiction, travel books, westerns, mysteries, war stories or true life adventure. It will be predominantly fiction; 'Literature is a luxury; fiction a necessity' as Chesterton remarked. He will constantly be making those comparative judgments within these categories which his studies of literature in a narrower sense have equipped him to make. He will be mindful that most of children's exposure to fiction today will be through the visual media rather than through reading and that the criteria on which these media are to be judged are only in part the same as those appropriate to books. He will, in the words of a familiar BBC slogan, strive to make the good popular and the popular good. Starting from where the children already are, their present tastes and interests, he will aim to help them to make similar discriminations between better and worse in literature and other media and to develop a positive preference for the better.

14 Why study literature?

I take it that the most obvious answer to this question will not do: for better or worse literature has become a subject in which there are examinations which it is desirable to pass.

An eloquent passage in the Board of Education's 1921 Report on *The Teaching of English in England* says of literature that it is the 'sublimation of human thought, passion, feeling', that it is 'concerned with issues which are of universal interest', that it 'introduces the student to great minds and new forms of experience' and is 'a means of contact with great minds, the channel by which to draw upon their experience with profit and delight'. In short, they argue that English literature must be as indisputably the cultural core of a liberal education for the mass of the people as classical literature had traditionally been for the élite. Matthew Arnold had expressed similar views half-a-century earlier and in the subsequent half-century they have been echoed by almost every writer on the subject, sometimes with fresh and inspiring conviction, sometimes, in school syllabuses, one suspects with flat sapience.

Plato had strong misgivings about literature and reluctantly banished poets from his Republic. He was so vividly conscious of how powerfully and pleasurably they could persuade us of the truth of their fictions that logic constrained him to see them as a threat to our ability to perceive the reality behind appearances. The sensible world was one remove from the true Forms or Ideas of things and works of literature were twice removed from reality. The Board of Education's insistence on the 'profit and delight' of literature is in direct line of descent from Horace's *'dulce et utile'*; he believed it should be sweet and pleasurable but also somehow useful. Renaissance critics following Aristotle and Horace rather than Plato, believed that literature's use was in supporting morality by holding up to man's eyes a vision of an ideal world which transcends the imperfections of the real world of human history, where the good often suffer injustice while the wicked flourish as the green bay tree. Subsequently, throughout history, the puritan temperament in whatever form it manifests itself has distrusted pleasure and when literature and the other arts with their undoubted pleasure have been permitted to flourish they have been expected to teach useful lessons, reinforce moral and religious truths, or support the current political and social ideology. Artists who failed these expectations were persecuted and silenced and in atheist totalitarian states today become the modern equivalent of the heretics and martyrs of old. When the pleasure of art is most suspect, satire commonly thrives because it can easily be justified – sometimes hypocritically as in the prefaces of bawdy Restoration comedies – for holding up vice and folly to ridicule and thus serving to correct morals and manners. In less puritan times the delight afforded by literature has needed fewer defences or been thought to be self-justifying: it may even be felt to release emotional tension in a harmless or even a beneficially cathartic way. Writers as different as Aristotle and Freud believed something like this.

Even if, privately, we believe the delight of literature to be self-justified, people who teach or study literature in educational institutions are often constrained to offer some further justification. What then is the further use or profit of reading literature? Few people today, one hopes, would suggest that works of literature should be used as the relatively unimportant means to the end of scholarly discipline. Some classical texts were once studied in this way and under that influence Shakespeare's plays and other English works have been taught in the same spirit: poring over the footnotes in 'the infernal Veritys' or subjecting poems to a systematic rhetorical and prosodic disembowelment was difficult and disagreeable enough to be regarded as the equivalent of construing Latin or Greek. Few people also, would want to make a major point of the fact that anybody who reads a good deal of literature is bound to pick up ideas and miscellaneous information. Such information, however delightful, is bound to be unsystematic and sometimes unreliable (think of Roman or fifteenth century English history as seen through Shakespeare's eyes). George Boas has said, too, 'The ideas in literature are usually stale and often false and no one older than sixteen would find it worth his while to read poetry for what it says.' Similarly, though it is one of the virtues of literary study that it constantly leads outside itself to non-literary areas, the knowledge acquired in seeking to understand a literary work – knowledge of history, philosophy or mythology for example – is likely to be piecemeal and partial. It could be argued that reading literature must widen vocabulary, provide models of excellence in language and a sense of style which beneficially affect the reader's ability to write effectively himself. This is probably true but, like other claims made for the benefits of literary study, difficult to prove. Literary critics and scholars do not all write in a way that lends it credence and a contrary argument might suggest that constant exposure to masterpieces of literary art might undermine the reader's confidence that he could himself write anything worth reading or find a style of his own.

The most far-reaching and important claims made for literary study are unfortunately the most difficult to substantiate. In *Education and the University*, F.R. Leavis is clearly conscious that exaggerated claims are voiced and make easy targets for sceptical critics of a literary education. He argues, nevertheless, that literary study at its best can be a discipline of intelligence and sensibility as well as of scholarly application and academic method. It should constantly involve judgments that are 'inseparable from that profound sense of relative values which determines, or should determine, the important choices of actual life'. If he is right, one cannot avoid the word 'moral' in describing the character and benefits of a literary education not, of course, that much literature, like fables, overtly and intentionally teaches moral lessons. Similarly I.A. Richards says that 'a steadying of judgment, an enhancement of responsiveness and understanding, a heightened sympathy and self-control' are often alleged to be the peculiar benefits of studying literature but he continues to ask, 'How often can an experienced teacher honestly say that these are, in fact, evident outcomes of the study of poetry and philosophy? How truthfully can anyone affirm that students of the humanities are more excellent human beings than others? These questions, I know well, are over-simple and perhaps unfair. I believe, nonetheless, that the discomfort they cause us has good grounds. Judged by standards we *still* know – though they may not rule examinations – English, as we teach it, does not do what it should. And even by the narrower examinable criteria, it does not make its students markedly and demonstrably better readers and writers, wider and abler communicators.' The discomfort caused by Richards's questions is increased by the thought that there is a smug, self-congratulatory narcissism in teachers of literature claiming that people with a literary education must have acquired increments of moral perceptiveness and sensibility that only literature can provide. 'Let me beg teachers to take a sane view of literature', said George Sampson, 'Let us have no pose or affectation about it. Reading Blake to a class is not going to turn boys into saints.'

Does all this mean that we can claim no more for the study of literature than that it provides the reader with unsystematic scraps of not always reliable information and stale ideas; that it exposes him to language used with precision and vitality which does not necessarily improve his own skill as a writer and that it gives a probably harmless enjoyment? Certainly, as Richards argues, we have no reason for complacency and should rigorously examine our directing implicit assumptions but this does not mean, I believe, that we should abandon too readily a faith that literature somehow improves people who read it which has undoubtedly inspired many good teachers. Recent writers have understandably been shy about asserting this faith. In the first place one would hardly expect literature to change people for the better in ways which were 'evident' if by this Richards means 'clearly recognizable or measurable' in the short term. No faith is supported by this kind of evidence. The belief that appreciative, sensitive response to a work of art, leads however deviously and uncertainly to a sensitive response to the needs of one's fellow men, makes it easier for us to imagine and sympathise with their feelings, is not of its nature likely to be amenable to scientific verification. But – other things being equal – it is not psychologically improbable that constant practice in imaginative response should lead to responsibility. After all, when we debate with ourselves what we ought to do in a moral and not merely a prudential sense, evidence and reasons are important but so is imagination; crucially we have to imagine the consequences of the various courses of action open to us. How will it affect X? What will Y feel? Imagination has the effect, as Coleridge says, of 'carrying the mind out of self' or is, to quote J.S. Mill, 'the power by which one human being enters into the mind and circumstances of another'. No wonder Wordsworth called it 'the mightiest lever known to the moral world'; moral responsibility is a matter of responding in an unselfcentred way with the heart as much as the head.

It may be that we are seldom confronted by those agonizing moral dilemmas which philosophers are fond of debating. We may not even, in practice, often have to deliberate consciously about what we ought to do in a moral sense, and for most of us most of the time, morality is more a matter of our instantaneous, unpremeditated actions and reactions of thought, word and deed. At this point it is, perhaps, worth returning to the idea of 'enjoyment'. The point about the enjoyment of literature is that it is not a mindless one, not simply the kind of escape from the difficulties and frustrations of our lives which most games, sports and escapist fictions provide. On the contrary, though it does take us out of ourselves and our immediate circumstances, it does so by making us extend our experience vicariously and imagine and realize something of the infinite variety and complexity of human nature and experience. And the enjoyment – indeed, the joy – of literature lies in this extension of our first-hand experience and this is true even, paradoxically, when the literature is tragedy: it puts our own lot in perspective. People who have access to this kind of joy are likely to be happy people and happy people do least harm in the world. Spinosa believed that, 'Happiness is not the reward of virtue, but virtue itself; and we do not enjoy happiness because we control our desires, but it is because we enjoy it that we are able to control them'.

All this may not add up to a proof of the moral value of studying literature that would satisfy a sceptic who persisted in asking I.A. Richards's questions; but such a belief is not a mere whimsical opinion either, like Coleridge's belief that a man who refuses apple dumplings cannot have a pure mind. There are at least rational grounds for believing what anyone who has experienced literature knows in his heart existentially, that the enjoyment of literature is a supremely worthwhile end in itself. Enjoyment then, is the central *sine qua non*: any other advantages which reading literature may have in conferring increments of sensitivity or moral perceptiveness, in extending vocabulary or general knowledge or a sense of style are secondary to and dependent upon enjoyment. C.S. Lewis has said, 'Those who read poetry to improve their minds will never improve their minds by reading poetry'. They put the cart before the horse for, as Dryden wisely remarked, 'poesy only instructs as it delights'. Students at any level, particularly the younger ones, who are required to read works of literature and do not take away from them memorably enjoyable experiences have not merely been unprofitably employed; they have been harmed. They will henceforth be less likely to expose themselves voluntarily to the influence of books which they suspect are regarded as literature and therefore boring or baffling. This is the great crime that teachers of literature are charged with by many if not most of the students who have passed through their hands.

15 Can literature be taught?

Clearly we can teach *about* literature. It is a body of historical material about which there are plenty of scholarly facts and theories. There are facts about the lives and times of authors, about literary forms and techniques, about changing taste and ideas: there are facts too, about works of fiction (which James Joyce called 'ficts'); about how many corpses there are at the end of Hamlet, about how Mr Bulstrode acquired his fortune in Middlemarch. There are theories designed to bind together and make sense of facts, about why certain forms or styles of writing predominated at certain periods, about 'who influenced whom to say what when'. All this material can be and commonly is taught like any other body of historical fact and can be tested relatively objectively: it is concerned with knowledge and either a pupil does or does not know the form of the Petrarchan sonnet; what fruit was embroidered on Desdemona's fatal handkerchief; or the influence of Robert Frost on Edward Thomas's work.

To teach and test this sort of information is not inherently more or less legitimate or problematical than to teach and test any other body of knowledge which makes up the bulk of the secondary school curriculum. However, anyone with a feeling for literature is likely to think the acquisition of this sort of information for its own sake misses the whole point and is an arid and stultifying occupation; lifeless knowledge lies 'bed-ridden in the dormitory of the soul'. 'The ultimate aim *at any level*', L.C. Knights has written, 'is that taking up into the self – not as inert possessions but as new powers – of insights embodied in all genuine literature'. It is conceivable, if unlikely, that someone with a scholarly knowledge of literary history might never have been personally moved by a work of literature. Teaching literature, it is felt, must be centrally concerned with notions like appreciation, enjoyment, response, insight, interpretation, critical discrimination and judgment. It is much less clear whether and how these less exclusively and straightforwardly cognitive capacities can or should be taught or tested. Indeed, it is often said that 'appreciation' – the key term – is caught rather than taught.

To take appreciation, enjoyment and response first, the teacher can give an account of his own response to a work of literature and this may be useful up to a point; his enthusiasm may be infectious. It is not a bad situation pedagogically for a pupil to wish to like what an admired teacher obviously likes, but there are serious dangers. Emphasis on 'appreciation' of great works inevitably suggests that the students are expected to admire all the material put in front of them, a sure method with the younger ones of stunting the growth of sincerity and discrimination. And as F.W. Bateson has said of English Studies in the University, 'as an educational method "appreciation" has the disadvantage of inserting the teacher between the work of literature and the undergraduate reader'. Where it fails, the student substitutes for any independent thought or feeling a garbled version of the teacher's account when he, in turn, is required to write about his response and no genuine appreciation has taken place, only a pointless and parasitic exercise in hypocrisy and imitation. Anyone who has marked a public examination in English literature has endured many teachers' model answers to anticipated questions at second hand only distinguishable from one another by being more or less successfully remembered or literately presented: the teacher virtually takes the examination by proxy. Requiring students to read certain critics and commentators is open to the same objection and abuse; hang-dog reproductions of standard literary evaluations, clichés of criticism, pirated eulogies from the textbooks and imitation-indignant castigation of faults are all too likely to result. It is doubtful if in any other subject the student is so persistently tempted and even encouraged to compromise his integrity as a reader and rewarded for acquiring an examination technique which negates the most essential feature of that subject's discipline. If there are grounds for anxiety at university level, how much greater should they be at O level with its tens of thousands of weakly motivated candidates taking English literature?

'Criticism' and 'appreciation' are virtually interchangeable terms in many contexts even if youngsters mistakenly sometimes think that 'write a criticism of ...' gives more licence to say unfavourable things. The trouble is that appreciation or criticism of great works of art, at least any evaluatory and interpretative activity that deserves the name, is a highly mature and sophisticated activity. At its best it requires a wrestle with words and meanings scarcely less exacting than the original act of creation and it is hardly surprising that most of the great critics have also been great literary artists. Indeed, as T.S. Eliot who is a case in point has said, 'the largest part of the labour of an author in composing his work is critical labour; the labour of sifting, combining, constructing, expunging, correcting, testing: this frightful toil is as much critical as creative'. Is it, then, quite unreasonable to expect students to verbalize their appreciation, their critical response? Eliot, again, has said mildly that 'It cannot be recommended to young people without grave danger of deadening their sensibility to poetry and confounding the genuine *development* of taste with the sham acquisition of it'. He concludes the same essay in *The Use of Poetry and the Use of Criticism* by wondering 'whether the attempt to teach students to appreciate English literature should be made at all; and with what restrictions the teaching of English literature can rightly be included in any academic curriculum, if at all'. There are, then, very serious anxieties that the 'appreciation' and 'criticism' work required of students which makes up a large part of literature teaching may be counter-productive and anti-educational – a sobering thought. And yet, isn't it also our experience that to be genuinely moved by a work and to attempt to express one's own perceptions and feelings about it can be a profoundly educative activity?

If we turn to interpretation, analysis, discrimination, some of the things that go on in literature classes may be scarcely less questionable. 'Comprehension' often becomes a bogey. The conscientious teacher understandably feels that for a class to read and fail to understand is intolerable and wants some assurance that they are comprehending what they read. Many books are fragmented and spoilt for younger students because the teacher keeps stopping and submitting them to a catechism of comprehension questions at a superficial verbal level, as if understanding were no more than the sum of a lot of separate acts of word-recognition. A pupil may understand a word, phrase or sentence as it passes by in its context quite well enough to follow the author's meaning, but to have to stop, look back and offer the teacher a synonym or paraphrase will often require a considerably greater degree of linguistic maturity than is needed to respond to the poem or story in a worthwhile way. Teachers should, I think, take considerable trouble to see that what they read is not too difficult in language, rely on their rapport with the class to sense if difficulties at this level do arise and throw in a hasty word of explanation where necessary, at all costs avoiding too much delay or giving the impression that the work of literature is being used as an excuse for a comprehension exercise. Of course questions of comprehension at a much more fundamental level will arise. If the class has been imaginatively engaged by what is being read, most of these will be raised in discussion by the pupils themselves, prompted sometimes by a question from the teacher aimed at uncovering an aspect of the author's intention, tone or technique, which they might have missed. Well phrased and strategically placed questions of this kind which lead to discovery, to seeing what is there for those who have eyes to see, is certainly an important part of what 'teaching literature' at its best might mean.

One hopes that the better and more recently trained English teacher will inflict on his pupils neither the rigour of an arid form of comprehension work nor the sloppiness of what Stephen Potter called, 'a littish, contemplative, nostalgic stew of "appreciation" '. He will very likely himself have been trained in techniques of close critical analysis often called 'practical criticism' in this country and 'explication' in America. Short poems or excerpts and prose passages, often in pairs for comparison, are studied without advance knowledge of author, date or critical reputation and conclusions must be reached about them independently and on internal evidence alone. In a class exercise or an examination question the unseen passage certainly avoids some of the worst features of the old essay-type answer on a set text and should discriminate better between more and less good readers. On the whole it has had a salutary effect on teaching and examining and has probably helped to attract intelligent students to the serious study of literature in sixth forms and universities. Three dangers need to be guarded against, however: practical criticism concentrates attention in depth on short extracts rather than building up the stamina to read and reflect on major works as a whole; it may develop a tendency to overvalue complexity and density of texture for their own sake; finally, techniques of analysis learnt in studying complex works may be quite inappropriate if applied to the relatively simple literature suitable for younger and less experienced readers. Hostile critics of practical criticism sometimes give the impression that it imposes a new threat to more traditional methods of teaching literature but over a century and a half ago Coleridge wrote, 'Instead of awakening by the noblest models the fond and unmixed love and admiration, which is the natural and graceful temper of early youth, these nurslings of improved pedagogy are taught to dispute and decide ... to hold nothing sacred from their contempt but their own contemptible arrogance – boy-graduates in all the technicals, and in all the dirty passions and impudence of anonymous criticism'. The important implication of Coleridge's remark for teachers is that children can admire and enjoy, long before they can or should analyse and criticise, that appreciation of literature can be real and rewarding long before the ability develops to make an ordered verbal response to it.

The prime business of literature lessons, it seems to me, is not analysis, criticism, discussion or any other kind of talk *about* literature, it is reading aloud or silently with enjoyment and, of course, re-reading. (Few experiences are sadder for a teacher of literature than to present a poem to a class only to be told, 'We've *done* that one Sir!') The greater the enjoyment and interest it generates, the more discussion, analysis and re-reading a piece of literature will sustain. If there is little pleasurable reaction detectable at first reading, it is usually better to pass on swiftly to something else rather than to persist and risk 'doing' it to death. This is a matter of the teacher's professional judgment. Enjoyment and enhancing enjoyment is his aim.

After enjoyment here and now and, indeed, through enjoyment, the teacher's aim is to influence children's reading habits and tastes hereafter. There is research evidence that the most important factor influencing those tastes and habits is the choice and availability of books. This suggests the most important sense in which literature can be 'taught'. Before the teacher is an authority *about* literature, an eloquent witness to its power to move him, a skilful analyser or asker of questions he has to be a chooser and provider of books and a presenter (introducer, public reader, performer, impresario) of literature. An impresario chooses the entertainment, sets the stage, settles the audience and focuses their attention, dims the house-lights, raises the curtain. His skill lies in capturing an audience and getting them alert, expectant, agog to share, not passively, in the performance. Today with tape and record, film and TV the teacher is not a sole performer but to 'teach' literature he still needs the skills of an impresario.

One other solemn point remains to be made. In most schools now, creative writing, drama and reading literature are complementary activities constantly cross-fertilizing each other. However, as James Britton has put it, 'As far as institutions of higher education are concerned, painting and music are things that you do but literature is something other people have done'. It is a highly anomalous situation. One might expect that the student of literature, the creative art of self-expression in writing, would be constantly practising that art himself and yet the truth is that from O level onwards, the ability to write better than merely grammatically hardly counts at all. English teachers may not be in business to train professional writers but their students at every level could use language creatively as part of their personal growth, quite apart from the fact that the surest way of appreciating an art is to practise it as an amateur. Yet students can and do pass out of universities and colleges of education as English specialists without ever having been required or even encouraged to compose anything other than literary, critical or historical essays. Good essays of that kind will be creative, of course, in the narrow sense in which good criticism and scholarship are always creative. Creative exercises in imitation or parody of writers being studied are not commonly used either, though they can often both lead to and reveal true insight and understanding. If it is objected that creative writing is difficult to assess fairly, it is odd, to say the least, that teachers who pride themselves on being good readers with trained critical acumen should be unable to solve this problem as satisfactorily as teachers of other arts. Interpretative skills, apart from critical exegesis, are as neglected as creative ones: the chances are that the student will never have had to read literature aloud to bring it alive to an audience or to take part in the production of a play in any capacity, however menial. If all students of literature were going to spend their lives as academic scholars and critics it might be possible to justify their conventional curriculum. All but a few, however, will enter teaching or some career where what I.A. Richards called 'wide and able communication' is of vital importance. Perhaps there is good reason to regret that English ever won the battle – historically so recent – for academic respectability. A.S. Neill was a student in the early days of the subject and although his reactions may not have been altogether typical they cannot be lightly dismissed as a cautionary tale. 'For four years I studied for exams in English, Old, Middle and Modern, Chaucer, Spenser, Shakespeare; dullest of all, Dryden. Professor Saintsbury had an unfortunate liking for Dryden, and we all had to pretend to an interest in Dryden. Today I could not read any of these writers; today I could not contribute anything at all to a discussion on post-Popian poetry or pre-Paterian prose ... A man should be awarded a degree for creative work. Instead of spending four years reading up what Hazlitt or Coleridge said about Shakespeare (I had no time in those days to read Shakespeare's plays), I should have been writing a play. To write a bad limerick is better than to learn *Paradise Lost* by heart.' (*The Problem Child*, p. 178.)

16 What kind of discipline does the study of literature involve?

So far I have not attempted to distinguish between studying literature and merely reading it. To speak of 'merely reading' is at once misleading: we may merely read office memoranda or much of the contents of a newspaper but, if what we have said about the nature of literature is true, it will engage our minds and hearts in a more comprehensive and personal way.

In one sense the discipline of studying literature could be summed up as good reading and we would then have to particularize what 'good' means in this context. We will return to this in a minute, but perhaps the student of literature, at an advanced level anyway, has to go somewhat beyond being a good reader. We could picture it to ourselves like this: the good reader is like the ideal passenger in a car being taken on a tour by the author-driver. He puts himself trustingly and unreservedly into the driver's hands, does not attempt to question his route or to be a back-seat driver, does not let his attention wander or day-dream but observes attentively what the driver wants him to see including, occasionally, the performance of the car itself. Keats's description of reading poetry as 'diligent indolence' perfectly suggests this combination of alert attention and relaxed self-forgetfulness which characterizes the good reader's surrender of himself to the experience which the author wants him to share. At the end of the journey the average passenger will depart gratefully, resolved, perhaps, to repeat his trip on some future occasion and:

> Contented if he might enjoy
> The things which others understand

The student of literature, however, will be less willing to depart in peace until he feels he fully understands. He will want to do at least three things. He will want to get out the map and retrace the journey he has taken pondering why and how the driver came to choose his route, took this turning rather than that and so on. Such questions may properly make him want to know more about the driver. Secondly he will want to open up the bonnet and inspect the vehicle, perhaps even take it apart to see how it worked to take him from starting point to destination, for the driver was also the mechanic who built the car. Thirdly, he will probably want to say something in his own words about the journey he has taken as a way of savouring, articulating to himself and thus beginning to understand the experience he has had. The more sophisticated he becomes, the more what he says will have some universality and not be a purely private reaction; he will speak for others as well as himself. Good readers in a perfectly legitimate sense of that phrase may be impatient with these further activities; they may even feel it perverse to want to take the vehicle apart rather than simply use it again as a delightful means of imaginative transport. He may, in any case, be anxious to get on and start another trip with the same or a different driver. This kind of good reader-passenger is, nine times out of ten, the sort that English teachers must prepare for a life-time of rewarding and memorable excursions. He should not be bullied into becoming a student of literature unless he shows a natural inclination to talk about his journey or get his overalls on, though he may occasionally listen and watch while we do these things: one can appreciate an enthusiast's preoccupation without sharing it and enthusiasts do have a way of becoming bores.

The *bona fide* student will be the best, most understanding, reader only if, when he put his map away and had his say, he puts the vehicle together again by a fresh act of self-surrender to the author's intention by re-reading his work. But, having said all this, is the 'good reading' of the student or scholar essentially different from the good reading of the amateur? I doubt whether it is. Of course we would expect the scholarly student, because he talks about what he reads, to acquire some technical vocabulary for describing different forms of literary work and the nuts and bolts of the writer's craft. His response may be no more sensitive than the amateur's and only more complete because he tries to articulate it. One would expect him to be more systematic in his reading and in relating one work to another and to its background as part of a developing tradition. One might expect him to read more literature from earlier periods and be prepared to tackle the obstacles such works inevitably present because of changes in language and in accepted ideas and beliefs. The amateur may be more attracted initially by twentieth-century literature – though this presents its own problems of interpretation and evaluation – and find it best to explore backwards from there.

Of course there is no clear dividing line between the amateur good reader and the professional literary scholar who may have spent a lifetime mastering a whole moral and intellectual culture very different from our own today, in order to qualify himself as a reader of Chaucer or Shakespeare or Johnson. There are simply more and less experienced and knowledgeable readers and it would be unrealistic for a scholarly teacher, whether he works in a school or university, to suppose that more than a few of his students all of whose lives can be immeasurably enriched by literature will have the same time or inclination for historical scholarship or background reading. He will need to distinguish carefully in his teaching between questions of historical importance, questions of aesthetic merit and matter of general and abiding human interest. *Gorboduc* may be of great importance historically as the first blank-verse tragedy in English but of little interest on the other two counts. It is all too easy for scholars to overemphasize the historical apparatus necessary for the understanding and enjoyment of the literature of the past and, as Stephen Potter noted in *The Muse in Chains*, to be tempted into antiquarianism, the belief that the past is good and fascinating *qua* past.

In the end, however, the good reader whether student or amateur, will read and reread and not judge hastily. He will have the humility to respect the judgments of readers more experienced than himself but also the integrity never to adopt their views without testing them out for himself. In the face of a great work that has stood the test of time he will realize that it is judging him as a reader more surely than he can hope to judge it. He will absorb himself in the writer's world without limiting preconceptions about literature or expectations other than the enjoyable sharing of that world. He will try to return works to the medium for which the artist intended them, to recite or hear ballads, to act or see plays, to sing or listen to lyrics. He will be adventurous in seeking new literary experiences and widening his taste. Above all, his reading will take on a pace and style quite different from the hasty skimming flight of the eye which the sheer volume of ephemeral or merely informative reading matter we have to consume tends to force upon us as a habit: he will read slowly, ideally aloud but, failing that, with sub-vocal articulation, hearing the author's words and the rhythm of his sentences in his head. His discipline, like that of all disciples, will lie in a willing submission to a master or a masterpiece.

17 Can literature be examined?

This question, more precisely phrased, means can we test by examinations whether or not our students have got out of the study of literature what we intend? Are examinations *valid* in testing what we want tested and are they *reliable* in fairly and objectively discriminating between the candidates? I have already said something about these questions in discussing whether literature can be taught. They have been hotly debated ever since English became a subject of academic study and formal examination and still cause much concern.

Information *about* literature, facts and 'ficts', can be taught, as we have said, in a straightforward way and there are no peculiar problems involved in examining candidates' knowledge about literature. Many O level questions unashamedly ask for 'ficts' and little more: ('Give an account in your own words of the wrestling scene in *As You Like It*' etc.) With more advanced students other relevant knowledge about literature is a reasonable requirement but, at any level, knowledge about literature is subsidiary to appreciation, taste, the ability to read perceptively and personal judgment and discrimination. Whether valid and reliable means of testing these capacities can be devised is a much more doubtful matter.

The authors of the 1921 Report on *The Teaching of English in England* were clear-headed up to a point: 'For good or ill', they said, 'the examination system is with us. To exempt literature alone from its scope would simply exclude the teaching of literature from a number of schools. Nothing less than the total abolition of the examination system would serve the turn of those who object to examinations in English, and to make such a recommendation ... would be entirely futile.' They continue, 'Many persons, doubtless, upon whose mind and character literature exercises an abiding influence, owe it to the examination system that they ever made acquaintance with literature at all'. This, it will be noticed, is very like the fox-hunter's defence of hunting, that it preserves the fox from extinction in a harshly competitive world of conflicting interests. They conclude, 'We are satisfied then, that in most schools the teaching of literature is bound to ally itself with the examination system. *Yet this alliance should involve no subserviency on the part of the teaching.*' As an example of naive optimism this last sentence would be hard to rival: any important public examination is bound to have a significant 'backwash' effect in schools and testing devices will dominate teaching methods leading to endless classroom practice of stereotyped examination tasks. About this, Fisher's Committee were less clear-headed.

Between the wars, anxiety over the effects of examining literature in the School Certificate increased. L.C. Knight's trenchant attack in *Scrutiny* (Vol. 2, No. 2, 1933) is a notable example. By 1941 the Norwood Committee were writing, 'We would assert our belief that premature external examination of pupils at school in English Literature is not only beset with every difficulty but is productive of much harm in its influence on the teaching of English literature and eventually upon English as a whole; for that reason we would advise against any such form of examination.' After more than thirty years and the replacement of School Certificate by the GCE the examination is still with us for the reasons the Fisher Committee saw so clearly in 1921 and there is little cause for optimism that its influence on teaching has become less harmful. Indeed, with the far larger number of candidates now taking O level and with English literature at around 220,000 candidates a year maintaining its position as third only to English language and mathematics, the harm, if it is real, must be more widespread. There has been no significant progress either, in integrating language and literature into a single examination as recommended by the Lockwood Report in 1964.

Briefly the argument against the traditional form of examination in literature might run as follows. In any examination which involves a large number of candidates and is to be reliable it must be possible to ensure a high degree of uniformity amongst a panel of examiners so that marks can be standardized. Unfortunately there is much evidence that in a subject like English (and this includes composition as well as literature answers) examiners' judgments of the same candidate's performance are notoriously variable and, indeed, an individual examiner may not be self-consistent. The only questions to which an objective marking scheme can be applied are ones which require facts or standard views. Questions which explicitly ask for candidates' own opinions are therefore usually a well meaning deception, as are rubrics which read 'Candidates should aim at appreciating the spirit of the books, their structure and style, as well as knowledge of subject matter'. (NUJMB) The questions capable of being marked reliably which can be asked on a set text are strictly limited and therefore highly predictable. Facts and accepted judgments, moreover, can be crammed by the candidate, sometimes at the last moment, sometimes without the text to which they relate ever having been read. The examination, therefore, can become little more than a memory test quite incapable of discriminating between the good candidate and the cunning examinee and the teacher is reduced to a tipster and dictator of specimen answers.

The problem is most acute at fifth-form level for several obvious reasons. A pass in Eng. lit. may be little esteemed by employers but thousands of candidates are put in for the subject not of their own choice but in the spirit of 'one more easy scalp to hang on your belt'. Schools and teachers are under great pressure to get as many through as possible since percentages of passes are avidly compared and taken as the acid test of educational efficiency. Moreover, the time available for literature in middle-school forms, as the Crowther Report noted in 1958, is likely to be the minimum considered necessary to cover the examination texts and this is quite inadequate for the wide and leisurely reading by which individual taste is formed. It is little wonder that Frank Whitehead has written, 'There is a deep internal incompatibility between external examinations as we know them and the essential aims of good English teaching'. The essence of the incompatibility is this: the discipline of English lies in thoughtful reading and re-reading and thoughtful writing and re-writing. The good student has learnt the difficulty of writing anything precise at first draft or of drawing worthwhile conclusions about his reading without reflection and re-reading: his training may have put him at a positive disadvantage in the race against the examination-room clock.

Even at university level, F.W. Bateson has confessed that in tutorials what don and undergraduate are cooperating in is often a private conspiracy to defeat an obsolete examination system. Among students, cynical advice passed on from one generation to the next can still pay dividends: memorize a judicious selection of your lecture notes and combine them with a few quotations from currently approved critics. Period papers can be passed and passed well in this way without texts having been read. While this remains true, it is scarcely constructive for tutors to express their irritation at a system only they have power to change by setting examination questions of the type said to have been favoured by W.P. Ker (*without* mentioning that he 'found it brick and left it marble' write something relevant about Dryden's contribution to English versification). Context questions at school or university level may test diligence more effectively than essay questions, but preparing for them may destroy enjoyment, deflect attention from what is central, involve a great deal of unprofitable labour in memorizing footnotes and an element of luck may significantly affect candidates' results. It is the only kind of question commonly set which would probably have to disappear (and a good thing too) if candidates were allowed their set texts in the examination room and this is, perhaps, why examiners have shown such otherwise inexplicable reluctance to make this highly desirable reform.

The picture I have sketched is a dismal one, but it would be wrong not to notice some chinks of light in the general gloom. I said in an earlier chapter that a good student should reveal something of his perceptiveness as a reader by his ability to comment on unseen passages of prose or poetry, particularly if the necessity for speed is reduced: practical criticism of this kind is now a part, and an increasing one, of many literature examinations. As a testing device it has two main disadvantages which need not completely invalidate it: it can lead teachers to devote a disproportionate amount of attention to small snippets of writing and also lead examiners in their search for passages that will be genuinely unseen by all candidates to unearth pieces of little merit or interest to anyone.

Secondly, mode three in the CSE makes it possible for course work written about literature to be marked internally by teachers and submitted to the examiners, with a guarantee that it is the candidates' own work, for moderation. The system may not be as incorruptible or susceptible to precise standardization as ideally a public examination should be, but confidence that it works fairly is probably growing to a point where it will be introduced at other levels. It certainly removes many of the worst 'backwash' effects of written examinations. In many universities and colleges now, course-work essays or dissertations count significantly towards final results.

Thirdly, examiners have become more adventurous in choosing works for study, particularly recent ones, outside the long established canon. Teachers, alas, are often reluctant to tackle a book that has not been set before or one that has not attracted much in the way of critical commentary. The tendency is a welcome one, however, even if it sometimes goes too far. A superficially attractive book which we would be happy for sixteen-year-olds to read may not have the quality to repay detailed study and re-reading whereas an initially less attractive text of indubitable literary merit may prove the more rewarding ultimately. The choice offered by GCE boards often poses a problem of this sort for teachers today.

Fourthly, some examiners have recognized the desirability of testing the breadth of a candidate's general reading. The main difficulty in making provision for this, I believe, lies in the problem of setting wide enough questions which are not as predictable and therefore susceptible to the prepared answer as those on prescribed texts.

Finally, some GCE boards now allow candidates at A level to submit some creative writing in verse or prose not done under examination conditions and endorse their certificates accordingly. This is certainly a small encouragement to those teachers who continue to make time for creative composition in sixth forms.

Despite these hopeful signs, examining literature is still beset by fundamental problems and perverts good teaching and study habits. Could a literature examination ever be both reliable and valid? It seems unlikely. It seems impossible to test the central concerns of literature teaching; enjoyment, personal imaginative response, taste and discrimination, even in this age of wonders by measuring glandular secretions, rate of respiration, blood pressure or electro-encephalograph, let alone by formal written papers. The dilemma must be faced. It is at least arguable that external examinations, if such there must be, would be more honest and less anti-educational in their effects if they set out to test only knowledge *about* literature and those reading skills revealed by practical criticism of unseen passages. Such knowledge and skills are at least necessary concomitants of reading with enjoyment and appreciation. Should they measure only what they can, not what they would and take the rest on trust? The only way so far devised (by Stephen Wiseman and others) by which composition can be reliably assessed without virtually ignoring subjective elements is to arrange rapid impression marking by a number of examiners of proven self-consistency whose marks are then aggregated and averaged. I do not know of instances where this has been tried on literature paper answers which are, after all, compositions in a proper sense of the word. Certainly examiners must now take more seriously than previously, the inevitable effects on teaching and studying in schools of any testing device just as their teacher-critics need an understanding view of the constraints of the examiner's unenviable task. Both teachers and examiners could do more to maintain that dialogue which is often woefully lacking. Examiners' reports are highly critical of schools and candidates and they receive in return more complaints and abuse than constructive suggestion. Neither is prodigal with praise of the other when there is evidence that the interests of literature are being well served.

18 What is poetry and how is it different from prose?

This book is not intended to provide a glossary of literary terms. A good one like the *Dictionary of World Literary Terms* (ed. Joseph Shipley, Allen and Unwin, 1970) will be constantly referred to by teachers and serious students of literature and a series like the *Critical Heritage* books (Methuen) will provide extended treatment of the specialist vocabulary of literary criticism. I only want to say here a few words about the distinction between poetry and prose because it is, I think, the most commonly raised, explicitly or implicitly, and the most persistently funked in the course of studying literature in schools. The question is a complex one and many thousands of books and articles have been devoted to it. What follows is only a sketch map to the semantic jungle that surrounds it.

Small children are brought up on nursery rhymes, songs and traditional jingles. These they are told are poems. When they first encounter verses that do not rhyme or rhyme irregularly they understandably feel that they are not proper poems. They have to discover that rhyme is 'no necessary Adjunct or true Ornament of a Poem or good Verse', as Sir Philip Sidney says. This is no great problem: we can show them blank verse or Hebrew poetry from the Bible depending on parallelism: 'The heavens declare the glory of God, and the firmament sheweth his handiwork'; or mediaeval verse depending on alliteration: 'In a somer seson . whan soft was the sonne, I shope me in shroudes . as I a shepe were'.

The next level of difficulty concerns verse and metre. 'Poetry', said Robert Bridges, 'selects certain rhythms and makes systems of them and these repeat themselves: and this is metre'. He appears to imply that metre or verse are *necessary* adjuncts of poetry and, of course, the words 'poetry' and 'verse' *are* often used synonymously but long before Bridges's day this had been disputed. Wordsworth, for instance, in his famous

Preface to the *Lyrical Ballads* had opposed poetry to 'matter of fact or science' rather than to non-metrical composition. Anyway, children will expect poems to look like verse on the page and to sound like verse by having regular repeating patterns. When they encounter some of D.H. Lawrence's poems or other examples of free verse and their expectations are not met they will, again understandably, feel that they are not proper poems. Are they not just prose arranged on the page in an arbitrary fashion instead of in ordinary sentences and paragraphs? What really is the difference between poetry and prose? The difficulty now becomes more complicated even if we can convince them that the arrangement of free verse is not arbitrary if it makes it easier for the writer's words to be read in the way he wants.

The root of the problem is this: any composition in *verse* is in common usage called a poem, whether it is felt to be good or bad. But if a composition in verse (a poem in this sense) does not affect us in a certain way we may feel that it is not poetry or not a true poem. 'Every man that writes in verse is not a poet', Ben Jonson said. Similarly if a composition in prose (as opposed to verse) or a part of one, does affect us in the way we expect of poetry we may say it contains poetry or is a (prose) poem. A well known critic, for instance, has said that much of Hardy's finest poetry is in his novels.

We use the words 'poem' and 'poetry', therefore, merely to describe any composition whose form is verse but also to denote the effect of something (usually words) on our mind and feelings, an effect we value. It is worth noticing that to call something 'poetic' would almost always be to praise it but to call something 'prosaic' would invariably be pejorative. The problem of meaning we have uncovered here is not new or unique. We have already seen that the word 'literature' too is used broadly descriptively for written or printed matter in general and also more narrowly and evaluatively. Words like this lead us into apparent paradoxes: we can meaningfully say that this poem (or piece of literature) is not a (real, true) poem (or piece of literature). The word 'education' is the same: we can say, 'He was educated at Rugby and Cambridge but I don't call that an education', though we appear to be asserting that he both was and was not educated – on the face of it a logical nonsense.

I said just now that it was 'usually words' we describe as poetry because the word can be used hyperbolically of other things; some buildings have been described as 'poetry in stone' (and 'frozen music', for that matter) and the flight of a bird or the grace of an athlete or dancer may be called 'sheer poetry'. This hyperbolic use is, in a way, very heartening because it indicates a recognition that, whatever else poetry may or may not be, it is something made or done with skill or artistry. It is not only heartening but also consistent with etymology for the word for the name 'poetry' in Greek meant 'making' and 'poiema' (work of art) was distinguished from 'logos' (logical discourse). The habit of equating poetry with verse though ancient does not go back to the origin but if poetry means, or has come to mean, something more than metrical composition, how can this something more be defined?

There have been countless attempts to define poetry and it is always easier to say what it is not than what it is, not science, not mere fact and so on. When it is defined by a poet, his attempt may throw interesting light on him and his work. When it is defined by a critic, it reveals the particular views or literary theories he held. To say that poetry is 'the spontaneous overflow of powerful feelings' or 'at bottom a criticism of life' or 'a morbid secretion like the pearl in the oyster' or 'adolescence fermented and thus preserved' may tell us something about Wordsworth, Arnold, Housman and Ortega y Gasset respectively. T.S. Eliot called poetry both 'superior entertainment' and 'a mug's game' and trying to define it also appears to be a mug's game because, as Eliot himself says, 'if our definition applies to *all* poetry, it becomes so general as to be meaningless'. It is, of course, writing or speech which is somehow special or different from ordinary everyday uses of language but there are plenty of other extraordinary uses of language – that of lawyers and stockbrokers – which no one would be likely to call poetry. The problem, then, is to define how it is different and this can be done by focusing attention either on the peculiarity of the language and content or on the peculiarity of its effect on us. The former which we will look at first is the more objective; the latter highly subjective.

Aristotle, focusing on content, described poetry as essentially mimesis (imitation or fiction). He was thinking of narrative and dramatic poetry and his view had numerous followers but only until verse was replaced by prose as the usual medium for drama and storytelling. He never defined lyric poetry but would probably have done so in terms of song and music rather than mimesis. (As the name implies, lyric poetry was sung to the accompaniment of the lyre.) Today we tend to think of lyrics (in the loose sense of poems which are usually short, personal and passionate) as being more truly and consistently poetic than narrative and dramatic poetry and even that narrative and dramatic verse is poetic in proportion to the lyrical elements it contains. This view makes poetry the condition to which all literature aspires and it is unambiguously expressed by Somerset Maugham: 'The crown of literature is poetry. It is its end and aim. It is the sublimest activity of the human mind. It is the achievement of beauty and delicacy. The writer of prose can only step aside when the poet passes.'

Other long-lasting theories defined poetry in terms of its use of lofty, grave, persuasive, ornate or highly figurative language but these all tended to confuse it with rhetoric or prophecy. Another ancient view associated poetry with magic and supernatural powers because of its ability to haunt and enthral the mind (Longinus's word was 'ecplexis'), its Phoenix-like ability to be reborn of its own consumption and its use in religious ritual and arcane practices. Turning to more recent centuries, Augustan theory saw the business of poetry as uttering memorably great truths which were common and general: the poet should not 'number the streaks of the tulip', Johnson said, and he could pick out the line 'Men have been great but never good by chance' as an example of poetry at its best. Since the Romantic revival, by contrast, the emphasis has been on the concrete and particular, on the uniqueness of first-hand experience and on personal feeling – feeling above all. Twentieth-century theories have tended to distinguish poetry in terms of its expressiveness or the complexity and compression of its communication. At the same time there has been a reluctance to talk about what a poem expresses, communicates or means. A poem *is* before it means; it is something made, a verbal construct which is *sui generis*, to be contemplated in and for itself rather than for any meaning or message that could be abstracted from it.

None of these views and theories exhaustively defines poetry or prescribes how the word must be used today but all of them can help to enrich the meaning of the word for us and the mysteriousness of that to which it refers. The meaning of a word, after all, is the sum of all the ways in which people in fact use it: there is no one right or proper meaning to be found in a dictionary or anywhere else and children's conception of poetry will widen to embrace new types of literary experience as they become more experienced readers.

It is difficult, then, and probably impossible to define poetry satisfactorily in terms of its characteristic content or use of language. 'The touchstone is emotion, not reason', says D.H. Lawrence. 'We judge a work of art by its effect on our sincere and vital emotion, and nothing else. All the critical twiddle-twaddle about style and form, all this pseudo-scientific classifying and analysing of books in an imitation-botanical fashion, is mere impertinence and mostly dull jargon.' It is easy to share the artist's impatience and to trust exclusively to our feelings, our gut-reactions. In the last resort, of course, that is what we all must do. I say 'in the last resort' deliberately because all of us must at times have been helped by analysis, discussion, critic-talk to recognize and appreciate poetry which we subsequently treasure but which, at first, made no impact on our vital emotions. 'Teaching' poetry is selecting and presenting poetry and the attempt to give that help. Marghanita Laski has spoken of the 'tear and shiver' test of poetry and it was said of A.E. Housman that he could never think of Milton's line 'Nymphs and shepherds dance no more' without tears. If this is true he was probably very unusual. The trouble with the 'tear and shiver' test is not just that it is non-rational and puts a stop to argument or that it is highly idiosyncratic and subjective but we are unlikely to be consistent in our responses: a line or poem (like a picture or a piece of music) may move us deeply one day but on other occasions we may not be in the mood for it. It too readily suggests a sentimental indulgence in wallow and gush. It is also quite inadequate to account for some of the loftier claims made for the power of poetry to transform men and enhance the whole quality of their living. 'We are shaken or lifted out of our ordinary state of consciousness. Many of our faculties are, for the moment, enhanced. We feel keener perceptions coming into action within us. We are given more than our normal stock of penetrative sympathy. We feel that we can enter into people's feelings and understand the quality of their lives better than ever before ... the whole adventure of mankind upon the earth gains, in our sight, a new momentousness, precariousness and beauty ... You feel as if new doors of understanding and delight were beginning to open around you. Some sort of mysterious liberation or empowerment seems to be approaching. You are assured, in an unaccountable way, that wonderful enlightenments, still unreceived, are on their way to you...' In this passage from *A Writer's Notes on his Trade* C.E. Montague is trying to fix and describe, as he says, the sensations that visit us while under the spell of poetry. If we did not know this, 'moral', 'mystical' or 'religious' would seem as appropriate words as 'poetic' or 'aesthetic' to describe the experience he is trying to put into words and it is not difficult to see how some people have found in poetry a substitute for religion or philosophy.

The *effect* of poetry is always a conjunction of object and subject, a particular arrangement of words with a particular mind and sensibility at a particular moment in time. The corporate act of sharing poetry in a classroom is therefore a chancy and difficulty business to manage. Like school assembly, but unlike a normal religious congregation or audience for a poetry reading, it is not a voluntary coming-together. One danger is that a teacher who has a deep personal reverence for poetry may fall into bardolatry or fly too high and neglect the lower slops of Parnassus. He mustn't forget the foothills by which he reached the heights or underestimate the sheer fun of the comic and curious or the sheer delight of sounds and rhythms. C. Day Lewis tells us in his autobiography, *The Buried Day*, how as a small boy the first bit of English that gave the authentic delight of poetry was an advertising slogan for a corset which read 'How to develop a beautiful bust', and he didn't even know what 'bust' meant. 'A poet is,' as W.H. Auden said, 'before anything else, a person who is passionately in love with language'. The opposite danger lies in what I once called Peter-pandering to puerility – insulting youngsters' sense of their own grown-upness by giving them wee folk, elves, wraggle-taggle gipsies and rosebuds when they have outgrown a taste for that sort of thing. I really did once hear a twelve-year-old mutter at the beginning of a poetry lesson, 'More hey nonny nonny and bloody daffodils'.

This chapter was not intended to answer the large and peculiarly fascinating question how to teach poetry. The aim was to sketch the problems of definition that reading and talking about poetry with children and students inevitably raise and which are often evaded because of their complexity. In particular I wanted to suggest how one might put them in the way of thinking about the difference between prose and poetry which would not turn out to be a confusing dead-end for them.

In his *Table Talk* Coleridge says, 'The definition of good prose is – proper words in their proper places; of good verse – the most proper words in their proper places'. With respect to the memory of a great man, this gets us nowhere. He is getting nearer the mark when he goes on to say that in poetry the *media* ought to attract your attention, whereas in prose for the words to attract attention to themselves is a fault. We could take this further with a passage in Stephen Spender's autobiography *World Within World* where he writes about pondering these questions of verse, poetry and prose. He concludes, 'Prose is language used in such a way that the ideas and events or scene within the language are referred to as objects existing apart from the language, so that there is an understanding between the writer and the reader that these things could be discussed in quite other words than those used, because they exist independently of the words. But directly the language tends to create, as it were, verbal objects inseparable from the words used, then the direction of the language is poetic. It is moving towards a condition where, as in poetry, the words appear to become the object, so that they cannot be replaced by other words than the ones used to convey the same experience.'

In other words, poetry is inherently unparaphrasable and the less adequately a piece of prose can be paraphrased without loss of meaning, the closer it is approaching to poetry. There can be no clear dividing line. Of course most poems do have a paraphrasable level of prose sense and this has to be attended to if we are to understand and respond to the poem as a whole.

Forty years ago I.A. Richards revealed in *Practical Criticism* what gross misreadings of poetry sophisticated students were capable of, even at this level. But to say what a poem is saying in any other words than those of the poem is to say something less than the poem says. Its total communication will be its prose sense *plus* everything that is conveyed by the sounds and rhythms of those words and their associations arranged in that way and in no other. This 'auditory level' of meaning, as T.S. Eliot calls it, may be the most important and certainly an indispensable part of the full meaning. Part of the aesthetic experience too, as with other works of art, will come from our recognition of the way the poet has shaped his material, the poem's formal qualities. Approached in this way, it is easy to see why paraphrase is such a dangerous exercise for inexperienced readers: it is likely to give the impression that the extractable sense of a poem is all that it has to convey to us and that poetry is therefore an ornate and confusing way of saying things which could more simply have been said in prose (if they are worth saying at all). And this is death to poetry.

It is a grievous reflection that, though most little children delight in rhymes and rhythms, they often leave school with an attitude to poetry somewhere between indifference and hostility. Arnold Bennett once remarked that the single word 'poetry' would disperse an English crowd more quickly than fire-hoses and part of the trouble is that as they grow up children catch something of the indifference or antipathy of their elders. The public stereotype of the poet is not so much the artist and skilled craftsman in handling words as a long-haired, loose living, effeminate and loquacious lay-about. The way poetry has been taught in schools cannot be exonerated from all blame.

19 By heart, by head or by rote?

Teachers of English still argue about whether or not children should be made to learn poetry 'by heart' and I have already suggested that one objection to traditional examinations in literature, as in other subjects, is the amount of unprofitable memorization involved for the candidates. There is a problem here, mainly of terminology, which needs to be sorted out in a brief footnote to what has been said in earlier chapters.

Let us start by allowing, as is customary, that the head is the seat of the intellect and the heart of the emotions. As all our lexicographers since Johnson recognize, 'learning by heart' is used as synonymous with 'committing to memory'. This is unfortunate: our language is blunt at a point where it is important, particularly for teachers, to distinguish sharply between different uses, abuses, methods and motives for memorization. In *A Plea to Boys and Girls*, Robert Graves makes a start:

> You learned Lear's Nonsense Rhymes by heart, not rote;
> You learned Pope's *Iliad* by rote, not heart;
> These terms should be distinguished if you quote
> My verses, children – Keep them poles apart –

Mere rote-learning has always been deplored: 'To fix in the memory without informing the understanding. Unintelligent repetition', says Johnson. Not so that drilling of the memory in information the use or significance of which is understood. This was often called 'learning by heart' but would more properly be called 'learning by head'. It is by far the most venerable and was until comparatively recently virtually the only known method of systematic learning. The meanings of 'learn' and 'memorize', certainly have a large area of overlap and it is clearly important, even if the importance has not always been recognized, for teachers and examiners to distinguish between the pupil who gives the right answer from rote memory and the one who gives the same answer but understands and therefore really knows it. Today most teachers would allow that there is still some place for 'learning by head' in the education of the intellect were it not that with the emphasis on learning through activity and experience all memorization tends to be equated with rote or parrot learning. So, in our reaction against the excessive verbalism of the past, confusion becomes worse confounded.

What, then, do we or should we mean when we talk about a child learning a poem 'by heart'? We mean committing it to memory, of course, but surely for reasons rather different from the ones that might prompt him to master his nine times table or the principal parts of an irregular verb. He *understands* that he *ought* to learn his tables or his verbs *if* he wants to be able to calculate or construe in his head. The imperative is hypothetical; it depends on the *if* clause and therefore a large part of the teacher's task is motivational. It is possible, as we all know, to learn poetry in the same conditional and utilitarian way – to impress an examiner, for example – but if we care for poetry we must feel that this has nothing to do with the true spirit. To 'learn by heart' should mean to memorize what the heart loves and desires to possess. We fall heart over head in love with a poem; we read it and re-read it until we have it by heart as a permanent possession; the memory grasps it readily and the learning is no labour. There is nothing calculating and conditional about the imperative 'I must have this'; the poem has intrinsic value for us and is not a means to some end.

There is one common experience that, to my mind, does the greatest mischief to our thinking about this whole subject. Many adults were coerced in their school days to learn large quantities of poetry, a task they heartily disliked at the time. When, however, they chance upon one of these poems in later life or an apt quotation comes to mind they feel a warm glow of affectionate recognition and gratitude to the teachers who made them memorize it. In this way they find an adequate justification for inflicting the same process on their pupils. I think we should challenge their reasoning by two questions. First, how many of them still read and memorize poetry, even occasionally, for their own delight? Secondly, how much of the feeling they profess for the poems they were made to learn at school is a pleasant nostalgia aesthetically quite irrelevant to the poems themselves? I have more than a suspicion what really honest answers would reveal. Anyone teaching a subject has to remember too, that he was probably an exception among his peers at school. He was good at the subject and his liking for it may have lasted in spite of rather than because of the way it was taught.

The IAAM handbook on *The Teaching of English* published in 1952 and reissued in 1966 contains this sentence: 'We must leave life to teach our boys what value to us remembered verses bring'. Should we not retort, quite simply, 'What is love? 'Tis not hereafter'. Isn't it through the heart, the seat of love, that the memory is safely reached without the danger of creating a lasting antipathy to poetry? It may well be that the young memory is more readily retentive than it becomes later in life. However that may be, the more poetry our pupils do 'learn by heart' the better. It is something that cannot be turned into a routine task regardless of individual attraction and preference: it must be an easy labour of love and then it will be the finest possible testimonial to the success of poetry teaching.

Unfortunately children are still made to learn and repeat poems, though less often now than formerly. Sometimes this is to help with examination answers; sometimes, one suspects, because it is a task to set younger children which does not produce a pile of exercise books to be marked. Too often recitation is a painful ordeal for all concerned: children mumble and stumble their way through and all too evidently the heart has played no part in the process of transmission to the memory. If the teacher was honest with his pupils he would say (adapting Shakespeare):

> Speak to the class
> Words roted in your tongue; bastards and syllables
> Of no allowance to your bosom's truth.

LITERATURE

Suggested further reading

BRETT, R.L. (1965) *An Introduction to English Studies* Arnold

DAICHES, D. (1956) *Critical Approaches to Literature* Longman

ELIOT, T.S. (1933) *The Use of Poetry and the Use of Criticism* Faber

HARDING, D.W. (1963) *Experience into Words* Chatto & Windus

LEAVIS, F.R. (1943) *Education and the University* Chatto & Windus

LEWIS, C.D. (1957) *The Poet's Way of Knowledge* Cambridge University Press

LEWIS, C.S. (1947) *The Abolition of Man* Geoffrey Bles

MAYHEAD, R. (1965) *Understanding Literature* Cambridge University Press

PEEL, M. (1967) *Seeing to the Heart* Chatto and Windus

POTTER, S. (1937) *The Muse in Chains* Cape

REEVES, J. (1956) *The Critical Sense* Heinemann

RICHARDS, I.A. (1926) *Principals of Literary Criticism* Routledge & Kegan Paul

RICHARDS, I.A. (1929) *Practical Criticism: a Study of Literary Judgement* Routledge & Kegan Paul

RICHARDS, I.A. (1955) *Speculative Instruments* Routledge & Kegan Paul

RICHARDS, I.A. (1973) *Interpretation in Teaching* Routledge & Kegan Paul

SHIPLEY, J.T. (ed) (1970) *A World Dictionary of Literary Terms* Allen & Unwin

SKELTON, R. (1963) *Poetry* English Universities Press

SKELTON, R. (1975) *The Poet's Calling* Heinemann

STEVENS, R. (1966) *An Approach to Literature* Longman

THOMPSON, D. (1973) *Reading and Discrimination* Chatto & Windus

WALSH, W. (1970) *The Use of Imagination* Chatto & Windus

WELLEK, R. and WARREN, A. (1949) *Theory of Literature* Cape

Imagination, Creativity and Self-Expression

20 What is imagination?

J.W.P. Creber said in the introduction to his excellent book *Sense and Sensitivity*, 'An essential part of the discipline of English teaching should be an attempt at a rigorous scrutiny of such a concept as imagination'. He goes on to outline an approach to English in secondary schools in which the personal creative writing of pupils is central and often leads into or grows out of encounters with 'imaginative' literature. This is splendid, but he does not, in fact, scrutinize the *concept* of imagination.

It is clearly a complex one: the dictonary defines it as the 'mental faculty forming images of external objects not present to the senses'. In this sense we can see that there can be excellent creative writing whether by pupils or by great poets, novelists or dramatists which does not employ images and is therefore strictly non-imaginative (like much non-figurative modern art). But the dictionary also defines it as the 'creative faculty of the mind' in which sense all creative work is imaginative. So imagination may mean, more narrowly, 'forming images' or as broadly synonymous with creativeness. This is only the beginning of the problem.

'The proper meaning of a word', R.G. Collingwood once wrote, 'is never something upon which the word sits perched like a gull on a stone; it is something over which the word hovers like a gull over a ship's stern. Trying to fix the proper meaning in our minds is like trying to coax the gull to settle in the rigging.' He is using imagination to express an abstract idea about semantics in the concrete terms of gulls, stones and ships just as the parable, the fable or the proverb do for religious, moral or merely prudential truths. The physicist does something very similar when he builds a model of an atom with coloured balls and so does the good teacher of any subject by giving examples, finding analogies, helping his pupils to picture in their minds. Analogies, images, metaphors used in this way are very helpful up to a point and even a necessary step in understanding; beyond that point they may have their dangers. A student who could not go beyond the model of coloured balls would be hindered in his understanding of the nature of the physical world just as a man who could not go beyond proverbial truths to see that 'circumstances alter cases' would hardly have begun to understand the moral world: Robert Frost's neighbour in *Mending Wall* could not see beyond his father's maxim 'Good fences make good neighbours'; 'he moves in darkness', Frost says.

For our present purpose, the problem with Collingwood's image is that words, like people, commonly have close relations within families. We not only have 'imagination' but also 'image', 'imagine', 'imaginative' and 'imaginary' to coax into the rigging; not one gull but a small flock of related sea birds; not one ship but a flotilla.

In the whole of our educational thinking, and not just in English, these words are clearly important. We speak with approval about imaginative teachers, syllabuses, lessons and teaching methods. In creative subjects like English, drama and art they are key terms; we encourage children both to respond to and produce imaginative work. But historians too, talk about developing the historical imagination, geographers the geographical imagination, sociologists the sociological imagination and so on. Even in science and mathematics the imaginative ability to hypothesize is now seen to be every bit as important as knowledge of facts and formulae.

I said that we use 'imagination' and 'imaginative' with approval and today they are words which have favourable overtones – pro-connotations as linguistic philosophers say. This was not always the case and it raises the first of a number of complications with which we need to wrestle. For a long time 'imagination' was generally associated with what today we would call 'mere imagination' or 'figments of imagination' and contrasted unfavourably with truth or reality. Thus Bacon called it 'the source of all folly, error, delusion and superstition' and said that 'it dazzles and snares the reason', while Johnson thought, 'All power of imagination over reason is a degree of insanity'. Macbeth imagines he sees a dagger before him and Lady Macbeth that there are spots of blood on her hands, though neither are there in reality: the hypochondriac imagines he is ill and the alcoholic that he sees pink elephants but they too are suffering from delusion, hallucination, false supposal; dagger, blood spots, illness and pink elephants are not there in reality but only in imagination and *imaginary* is the appropriate adjective for them. It is not difficult to see why imagination had a bad name or why Shakespeare coupled the lover and the poet with the lunatic as being 'of imagination all compact': if one has a strong imagination, 'How easy is a bush supposed a bear', how easily is one deluded into false supposal.

Clearly it is important at this stage to distinguish between things which happen in imagination *voluntarily* and *involuntarily*. The *in*voluntary imagination may be a serious degree of insanity or a harmless bubbling up of the subconscious as in dreams and day-dreams: dreaming when we are asleep, indeed, is now thought to be an important precondition of mental health in our waking lives and the hypnogogic images that float and collide in the mind in day-dreaming are now attracting attention from psychologists as the possible source of creative inspiration. There is the familiar story of the great chemist, August Kekulé, seeing as he dozed chains of molecules like snakes wriggling around. When one of those snakes grabbed its own tail it gave him the clue to the benzene ring, a major breakthrough in chemical theory and he said in 1890, 'Let us learn to dream, gentlemen, and we may find the truth'. It is often impossible, of course, to distinguish between the imaginings of the creative genius and of the mere dreamer or madman but all of us are problem-solvers at some level: when we find it helpful to 'sleep on a problem' we are making time for our imagination consciously and unconsciously to explore its ramifications.

The ability *voluntarily* to give imagination free reign is of very great educational significance. Children have it in abundance as we can see from the 'let's pretend' of their play and they can often be miles away in imagination when they appear to be attentive in the classroom. One of the fascinating things about their writing and painting is that we can often see beneath the surface their exploration of aspects of the adult world which they find perplexing or alarming and it remains true for all of us that we may first begin to explore the reality of ourselves and the world around us in imaginary or symbolic form, before we can approach and understand it explicitly and literally. Reading and writing in English give scope for that imaginative exploration. What we are coming increasingly to understand is that the creative adult combines the child-like ability to play freely with ideas in imagination with the ability to test out and evaluate those ideas against reality in the process of problem-solving.

I am out for a walk with my small boy when we find a plank lying on the verge beside the road and he says, 'Daddy, can we take it home?' I imagine how it got there: fell off the back of a lorry, perhaps. I imagine how heavy it would be and how far we would have to carry it. I imagine what we could do with it if we took it home: mend the fence, saw it up for firewood. My imagination is working at a practical, reality-adjusted level. In fact, when the plank is deposited in the garden, it becomes a see-saw, a race track for model cars, a space-ship, a stockade behind which Indians crouch and a property in other games. In the fantasy world of the child's play, the imagination is working in a more freely associative way. It could, moreover, be play conducted with or without much imagination: when the plank becomes a stockade or a covered wagon the play could be a stereotyped 'Bang, Bang, you're dead' or elaborated into a minor work of dramatic art.

We will return to the uses of imagination presently but for the moment there are other complexities in the concept to be brought into focus.

Just as words exist in families, so do images. We may tend to think of imagination primarily in visual terms as a mental picturing. This is understandable because for normal human beings, sight is the most acute and indispensable of the senses and it is not surprising that we have the common word 'visualise' for imagining or seeing in the mind but no comparable words for hearing, tasting, smelling and touching in the mind. Yet images can be auditory, gustatory, olfactory, tactual or kinaesthetic as well as visual. To take an example used by Kant, we might be walking down a street on a cold night and see a warm glow coming from a curtained window of a house. We could imagine (visually) a fire burning cheerfully in the grate but we could also imagine (auditorily) the sound of logs hissing and crackling, (olfactorily) the smell of the smoke or of someone making toast and (gustatorily) the taste of the toast. We could also imagine (kinaesthetically) as we stood in the street the physical movement of crouching by the hearth and (tactually) the feel of the warmth on our hands. All that our senses actually perceive is the sight of the curtained window but these other sensory images might pass through our mind with great vividness. Kant realized that they could all be present in the mind simultaneously; they tend to cluster together in what he called a 'manifold' or 'transcendental synthesis'. No two people in that street, of course, would necessarily notice the same things in their surroundings or imagine in the same way if they did. An artist can select and control our imagining more closely. If we suppose two tramps both catching sight of the curtained window, the one well fed but cold, the other warm but very hungry, it is possible, to put it no higher, that the first might imagine most vividly the warmth of the fire, the second a table spread with food. Images are linked not just with our five senses but also with our feelings. Strong feelings arouse vivid images and, vice versa, vivid images can arouse strong feelings. This is why the artist concerned with the emotional as much as the intellectual part of our lives relies more heavily on images than the scientific writer and why talk of 'imaginative literature', though misleading, is only marginally so.

A further complication in using the word 'imagination' arises from three different levels of its operation in the conscious mind which we might call primary, reproductive, and secondary or creative. The primary imagination Coleridge called 'the living power and prime agent in all human perception'. Most earlier philosophers up to and including Locke and Berkeley had thought of the mind as a passive blank page (*tabula rasa*) upon which images from the senses were imprinted. The insight which was new among philosophers in Coleridge's day was that what the mind receives is merely sense data, light and sound waves of certain frequencies and so on, which it has to interpret and construct into the objects of the external world. From where I am sitting now, I do not see a table before me, only a bundle of visual stimuli: its top does not look rectangular or horizontal from this angle and I can only see two of its legs. My mind, drawing on past perceptual experience and synthesizing it, interprets these visual stimuli as an object called a table with certain properties such as a rectangular top and four legs. Similarly my ears are receiving a distant tapping sound but it is my mind which interprets it as a secretary typing in her office. The mind therefore is active not passive all the time in the very act of perceiving the world; this is Coleridge's point; it is unique and individual and selective in the reality it constructs and it can misinterpret the signals which it receives when they are inadequate or ambiguous as in the case of optical illusions.

By the reproductive imagination we mean simply memory and in many contexts 'imagine' and 'remember' are synonyms. This is the source of much possible ambiguity. 'Imagination and memory are but one thing', says Hobbes, 'which for diverse considerations hath diverse names'. If I say to you, 'Imagine the room in which you slept last night', I mean recall to mind, remember. Go on: open the door. What do you see in front of you? ... to the left? ... to the right? Where is the bed? My questions, because we are language-using animals, can lead you to break the space/time barrier and, in J.S. Mill's phrase, 'conceive the absent as if it were present'. Stephen Spender says, 'It is perhaps true to say that memory is the faculty of poetry, because the imagination itself is an exercise of memory. There is nothing we imagine which we do not already know.' This cannot be the whole story because we all remember but are not all poets. Dryden saw the faculty of imagination in the poet as 'like a nimble spaniel (which) beats over and ranges through the field of memory till it springs the quarry it hunted after'. The imaginative writer's mind in the act of creating is trained and disciplined to be swift, selective and precise. We can often help children (or adults for that matter) to bring to life a piece of writing out of first-hand experience by encouraging them to imagine or remember clearly, and not in visual terms only but also by asking questions such as: 'What did it sound like, feel like, smell like?' What Spender's remark quoted above does not indicate is that the imagination of the poet does not merely reproduce what he remembers but, in a real sense, reconstructs or recreates it. In practical as well as expressive contexts too, imagination, to quote a psychologist, F.C. Bartlett, 'enables us to pick bits out of the mass of past stimuli, compare, condense and combine them, and use them to solve today's problems'.

The field of memory or imagination is confined, as Spender says, by the limits of our knowledge or experience: part of the case for reading literature or watching plays or films is that it extends that experience vicariously, but imagination is certainly not confined to reproducing what we have experienced at first or second hand. The creative or originative imagination which Coleridge called the secondary imagination 'dissolves, diffuses, dissipates in order to recreate'. There are simple memory images but also created images: you can imagine your actual bedroom but also the bedroom that ideally you would like to have. You can imagine the kettle you have many times seen boiling on the stove but also the possibility of using that steam to drive an engine. When we speak of imaginative literature or science, or simply of an imaginative person, it is to the secondary imagination, this creative ability we all have in some measure to freely reassemble the images of memory into new combinations, that we refer to. Drever's Penguin *Dictionary of Psychology* indicates this distinction between the reproductive and creative imagination and then goes on to make a further distinction: 'Imagination: the constructive, though not necessarily creative, employment of past perceptual experience, revived as images in present experience at the ideational level, which is not in its totality a reproduction of past experience but a new organization of material derived from past experience. Such construction is either *creative* or *imitative* being creative when self-initiated and self-organized, and imitative when following a construction initiated or organized by another.' The novelist imagines creatively the fictional world of his characters and plot; the reader following him imagines them imitatively, though all these distinctions are relative and would need endless qualification.

One facet of imagination at both the creative and imitative level of particular interest to English teachers, as I have argued in the chapter 'Why Study Literature', is its possible sympathetic, empathetic or moral implications. There is no need to say much more about this here. 'This is the power', said Mill, 'by which one human being enters into the mind and circumstances of another'. Now any good teacher, of course, needs to select, present and explain his subject matter in a vivid, memorable, imaginative way but to do this he needs to see that material, the difficulties it presents, and, indeed, his own performance as a teacher through the eyes of his pupils – to put himself in their place. The English teacher in so far as he is sharing with pupils the fictional world of writers is at an advantage: it is already imaginatively structured though he, like any other teacher, needs imagination to select and present it to the best advantage. In encouraging his pupils to enter into that imaginary world and its characters he may believe or at least hope that their capacity for sympathetic identification with their fellow human beings may be enhanced. Their imaginations are being exercised and as Mrs Oliphant, the Victorian novelist, said 'Imagination is the first faculty wanting in those that do harm to their kind'. In the previous century which was, if anything, more conscious of the dangers than the benefits of imagination Dr Johnson said, 'All the joy or sorrow for the happiness or calamities of others is produced by an act of imagination, that realizes the event ... by placing us, for a time, in the condition of him we contemplate, so that we feel ... whatever emotions would be excited by the same good or evil happening to ourselves'. Whether the capacity for such imaginative self-identification with others is innate and whether it can be developed by reading literature is a crucial empirical question but one about which it seems impossible to obtain conclusive evidence.

Today in the whole of education, and English teaching is no exception, we can detect signs of a shift of emphasis away from memorizing information and learning some traditional skills, towards the encouragement of creative, imaginative thinking. The reason is not far to seek. We now have a technology growing more sophisticated every year which can store and retrieve information far more efficiently than the human brain and machines which can be designed and programmed to perform many tasks which previously required a craftsman's skill. There has been gain and loss inevitably. But though large claims are made for the actual and potential capacities of computers, it seems fair to assume that they could never replace the creative artist, scientist or inventor. Throughout history, inventive, imaginative people have cropped up endowed in large measure with those creative abilities we all have to some degree. We do not know much about their originality, how far it depended on endowment, inspiration, perspiration, preparation, encouragement or happy chance. Today we have the opportunity and the challenge of releasing and fostering the creative potential of everyone as never before.

21 Created creative?

In looking at the development of English as a subject, we saw how ideas of creativity and creative self-expression have re-emerged as central to thinking about English teaching in the recent past. What is the background to this shift of emphasis? Are all our pupils potentially creative? What do we mean by creativity? Can we expect creative work in English from all pupils and if so, what is its value?

In the last chapter it emerged that there is a large area of overlap between the meanings of 'imagination' and 'creativity'. We all construct our own reality out of sense data and to that extent create rather than merely receive our images of the world, (although today, of course, some of these pictures of the world are processed for us and come second hand through the mass media). Much of the everyday thinking that all of us do employs images in a way that is creative in a perfectly proper sense of the word. Coleridge saw that at this primary level our use of imagination is 'a repetition in the finite mind of the eternal act of creation in the infinite I AM'. Whether God created man in His own image, as many religions assert, or men have created their gods in their own image as the sceptical student of comparative religion might tend to conclude, the necessary implication is clear: man is basically and by nature himself creative. Until recently, this implication has seldom been given much emphasis in religious teaching and the reason is not far to seek. Just as in the whole of education children were traditionally expected to acquire knowledge from authority, so the churches insisted that they acquire their beliefs from authority and their moral standards too. Individual creative thinking in these areas would be disturbing and potentially disruptive and dangerous. Much of the ferment in contemporary education and social life generally, which is sometimes ascribed to decadence, loss of direction and despair about values, may be interpreted more optimistically as a symptom of an exciting and perilous revolution which, bit by bit, is ousting traditional authority from the central position it has occupied for centuries and replacing it with individual responsiveness, responsibility, creative thinking and personal discovery. If the 'new morality' means anything more than an unprecedented permissiveness in sexual ethics, it is a reaffirmation of Kant's insight that to be moral, human beings must be autonomous moral agents creating the law they obey.

The English teacher, as we have seen, is inescapably concerned with values, often specifically moral as well as aesthetic ones. He may once have imposed values on children, or tried to, as an arbiter of right and wrong in matters of language and as the shepherd who drove his docile flock up the slopes of Parnassus. Today, if he is wise, he knows he can only explore values with children, teaching them not what to think but how to think, and that mere obedience to rules does not make good writers or readers.

Unfortunately, to assert that all people are or ought to be creative in the Coleridgian or Kantian sense, though importantly true, does tend to rob the concept of any further meaning. Many 'progressive' English teachers, deeply though not always clearly committed to the notion of equality in some sense and constantly confronted by evidence that their pupils are not all equally intelligent or able to cope with academic studies, may have tended to think of them as at least equal in their need, and perhaps also in their potential capacity, for creative self-expression. What can psychology tell us about this?

Certainly there has been an explosion of interest in creativity since the late 1950s and a great deal of psychological research has been devoted to the problems of identifying individuals of high creative potential and devising educational programmes and conditions of work that will develop rather than thwart that potential. In the sciences, engineering, industry and administration, even in the armed services, much attention has been paid to the need for creative, imaginative thinking. The concern is not primarily with artistic production nor with the satisfaction and well being of some exceptional individuals; rather the economic strength and even the power to survive of whole nations in a competitive world is what is now seen to be at stake. Open-ended tests of creativity or divergent thinking show wide variations in performance between individuals. Unfortunately the words 'creative' and 'creativity' tend to be used in conflicting senses not only by laymen but among psychologists themselves. Sometimes they call an individual creative if he scores highly on an open-ended test, sometimes only if his performance on such a test is significantly better than his score on a 'closed' test of intelligence where there is one right answer to each question. In either case the psychologist recognizes that a high creativity test score does not ensure creative *achievement*: for that, additional personality factors may be crucial such as persistence, self-confidence and the capacity for self-criticism. There is still no convincing evidence that children who score highly on open-ended tests are necessarily the most creative children in practice. As so often happens, at the end of the day when the social scientist has had his say, the teacher is a little wiser.

As far as English is concerned, one's own language is the most obvious and readily available medium in which to be creative. Collections of selected children's writing show that some of them have literary gifts of a high order; this is not in dispute, but what about the majority? Opinions differ. At one extreme, a student of mine was recently rebuked by a senior English teacher under whose guidance he was working for proposing to set his class an imaginative composition to write. They were an unimaginative lot, he was assured, and anyway it would be a waste of time since they would have no occasion to use a pen when they left school in two years' time except to fill up forms and write an occasional letter and were consequently better employed practising these useful skills. This teacher is not unique and his type of emphasis on a limited, utilitarian literacy is often welcomed by other subject teachers and praised by employers. There really is a chasm between this approach and the belief shared by many other English teachers today that all children can and should be encouraged to use language creatively; that they are all poets, novelists and dramatists *in posse* if not *in esse* and that they will incidentally be able to cope with all the demands made by society for a bread-and-butter literacy hereafter if English lessons are devoted to creative communication about things that really interest and

implies that other writing, particularly criticism, is destructive – though I still have pupils who, having concentrated their intelligence and seriousness upon evaluating a writer who matters to them, will refer to their work as mere criticism, as against the real thing, the formless verse they toss off in idle moments'.

Anyone who has watched and listened to young children knows that they are constantly creative and inventive in their play with any material, including language, that is at hand. Martin Buber, the great Austro-Jewish theologian, detected in man two basic and autonomous instincts: the first is the gregarious instinct for communion or 'mutuality' and the second is the solitary instinct of creativity or 'origination' as he called it. This creative instinct, he argued, could not be reduced, as some psychologists suggested, to the 'libido' or 'the primal will to power'. 'Here is an instinct', he said, 'which, no matter to what power it is raised, never becomes greed, because it is not directed to having but only to doing; which alone among the instincts can grow only to a passion, not to lust; which alone among the instincts cannot lead its subjects away to invade the realm of other lives. Here is pure gesture which does not snatch the world to itself, but expresses itself to the world.' How does this instinct of origination most readily express itself? Buber's answer is clear: 'Art is the province in which a faculty for production, *which is common to all*, reaches completion. Everyone is elementally endowed with the basic powers of the arts; these powers have to be developed, and the education of the whole person is to be built up on them as on the natural activity of the self.'

For many teachers of the arts, including English, Buber here provides a positive credo. Every known culture has developed art in some form, as surely as it has developed language. From palaeolithic times onwards, before the birth of agriculture, architecture or industry, simultaneously, perhaps, with the emergence of myth and religion, man has painted and carved, danced and decorated, and made images of natural and supernatural creatures and the earliest surviving writings in many languages are poems. It is odd that an activity as fundamental to all known cultures as art should in our own day have become peripheral and often passive in education and life.

Much has been said about the way children's natural creative, artistic expressiveness tends to go underground with the increasing self-consciousness of adolescence, often never to re-emerge. Much has been said too, about the increasing destructiveness with which many adolescents express themselves so that vandalism is a major social problem. It seems important to juxtapose these two observations. If the basic instinct of origination is thwarted, frustrated, neglected, it may well turn to destructive ends or so Erich Fromm believed in his *War Within Man* which he sub-titled 'A psychological enquiry into the roots of destructiveness'. Another writer and teacher, Sylvia Ashton-Warner, saw the child's mind as 'a volcano with two vents; destructiveness and creativeness. And ... to the extent that we widen the creative channel, we atrophy the destructive one.' Certainly where creativity is denied, the whole life of the person is stunted, particularly in emotional growth, for the prime function of art, underlying even its most playful manifestations, is to objectify feelings so that they can be ordered, contemplated, understood, shared and enjoyed.

If the submergence of creativity is in part a concomitant of a natural stage of development, its failure to re-emerge is a tragedy for which education cannot escape a large share of the blame. As far as language is concerned, education increasingly emphasizes what Robert Graves calls 'the cool web'; a logical, propositional, transactional language at the expense of personal, expressive and poetic modes. Even English teachers may tend to emphasize balanced discussion *about* feelings in studying literature rather than the direct expression of first-hand emotion. All too often creative writing is left behind in the latter years of compulsory schooling in favour of narrowly utilitarian tasks and practice runs at examination answers. Creative work in schools, Raymond Williams says, is widely regarded as *play*: 'This means that at a certain age it can be dropped, and put away with other childish things. It is indeed play in the sense that most of us enjoy doing it. But these creative activities are also forms of work ... In the changes that come with puberty it is vital that the practice of these activities should be continued, with no setting of "more real" or "more practical" work above them.' Even of those who stay in full-time education beyond the leaving age, the majority, if they get any English at all, are unlikely to be encouraged to write creatively: the minority who specialize in English will find the subject becomes a corpus of literary texts to be studied for examination. After the fifth form, as we said in an earlier chapter, the ability to write better than merely grammatically seems scarcely to count at all and literature, unlike the other arts, becomes something other people have done rather than something you do. It would be ludicrous to imagine a student of art (who might well go on to become a teacher) never handling a brush or pencil: similarly a music student who never practised composition or, at least, exercises in harmony and counterpoint and who was never required to play his instrument is unthinkable. Yet the higher education of the future English teacher is of precisely this kind. The chances are that he will never be required and seldom even encouraged either to perform literature in a way that might bring it alive to an audience or to practise it himself except in the form of literary critical and historical essays.

There are many reasons for deploring this situation. For one thing, the surest way to appreciate and understand an art is to try practising it oneself. For another, it is all too easy for the person with a literary education but without the constant humbling discipline of creative endeavour to fall into a complacent, élitist, narcissistic belief in his own superior taste and refined sensibility, even his own moral and spiritual superiority. Many defences of a literary education are shot through with a concealed narcissism of this kind. Both literary and linguistic studies tend to drift into antiquarianism when they are divorced from the living experience of trying to make something new. The teacher who, through lack of practice, has lost confidence in his own capacity to use language creatively, who has lost the habit of hoarding and recording his own thoughts, feelings and moments of vision, who no longer has the inclination simply to play with language and see what happens, is at a disadvantage, to put it no higher, in attempting to elicit creative work from his pupils. But we can at least end on a hopeful note: mature men and women who have never attempted to write a poem or a story since their own earlier school days can surprise themselves and others by the imaginative power they find they still possess if they are given the right encouragement and opportunity. A basic instinct may lie dormant but isn't dead. This was impressively demonstrated in the work produced by a group of experienced English teachers in Frank Whitehead's heartening little book, *Creative Experiment*.

22 What sort of self-expression?

In the last chapter I suggested that not much of children's writing will be creative in the sense of inventing a fictional world; rather it will be creative in attending to the sensuous quality of the everyday world, matching words to first-hand experience and thus expressing those individual impressions, feelings and ideas. Self-expression is, therefore, a central idea in the English teacher's thinking about his job. The same, of course, is true for art, drama and, to a lesser extent, perhaps, for music; indeed, they have been called the 'expressive' subjects to distinguish them from other areas of the humanities curriculum. Although self-expression is often cited as *an* aim if not *the* aim of these subjects, it is a tricky notion that needs a good deal of analysis if it is not going to be the source of much confusion.

Clearly not all forms of self-expression are equally acceptable socially, or valuable educationally. A group of bored and frustrated youngsters may express their feelings by vandalising a telephone kiosk or breaking windows. They presumably feel temporarily better after letting off steam in this way. This form of self-expression is obviously unacceptable because it is destructive of public or private property. We may conclude that self-expression which makes, rather than destroys, must be more valuable and in general this is probably true though one can think of constructive actions, like drawing an obscene picture on a public wall or writing a poison-pen letter, which would be as unacceptable and illegal as destructive ones. By concentrating on the social consequences for good or ill of self-expressive behaviour, we may deflect attention from what is educationally speaking, a more immediately relevant question, namely, what are the consequences for the person expressing himself? Is his self-expressive behaviour merely *reactive* like turning a cartwheel for joy or swearing when he hits his thumb with a hammer (and wrecking a telephone box is merely reactive in this way)? Is it, on the other hand, *self-reflexive*? In other words, does it turn feelings into a symbolic form that enables them to be seen, known, understood and controlled? Feelings and sensations can only be *known* in this way and to express a feeling in language or some other medium is to have objectified it and probably to have dissipated its controlling power over us. One of the features which distinguishes the educated from the uneducated or half-educated man is not so much a matter of his intellectual agility or emotional sophistication or the information he possesses as the degree of his *self-consciousness*, the ability to look with some detachment and objectivity at his own thoughts and feelings. This thought prompts us to look next at the way 'self-expression' is often linked to and contrasted with 'communication'.

In an earlier chapter, I suggested that English is like Art in being essentially concerned, not so much with a body of knowledge, as with skills of expression and communication. In both subjects there can be differences of stress depending on which of these terms, 'expression' and 'communication', is emphasized. One teacher may stress stimulating and exploring feelings, emotional development through creative expression; another, concerned with communication, may emphasize skills and craftsmanship rather than creativity. This could result in an insistence on neat literacy and the logical arrangement of ideas and argument in the case of English, or accurate draughtsmanship and other technical accomplishments in the case of art. To put it another way, one could say that the first teacher is more concerned with the *subject*, the person, that is, and the individuality of the ideas and feelings expressed, the second with the *object* produced, writing, painting or whatever, and the control of the medium displayed in its making. These differences of emphasis are real enough and make real differences to classroom practice but we should not hastily conclude from this that there is a clear dichotomy, a real either/or choice between expression and communication. Every instance of communication implies that something has been transmitted; at the least that an act of expression has been received and at best that there has been a mutual exchange of messages between two or more people. Is it also the case that, conversely, an instance of self-expression implies an act of communication? This is a more difficult question and, on the face of it, the answer seems to be no. Self-expression implies a giving out but not necessarily a taking in. Artists have often claimed to produce their work out of an inner compulsion to express themselves and that whether anybody will comprehend or appreciate their work is a consideration of total irrelevance at the time of creating it. As C. Day Lewis says of poets, 'We do not write in order to be understood; we write in order to understand', and another poet, Richard Wilbur, says that making a poem is 'a conflict with disorder, not a message from one person to another'. A few but not many artists, I believe, have kept up a creative output in total isolation and secrecy: some seem to have been genuinely indifferent to popular reaction to their work but nearly all of them have depended on communication with a small group – fellow artists perhaps – whose judgment they valued. It is unlikely that many people could sustain a creative activity with no reassurance that their work was communicating and being appreciated. A work of art, in whatever medium, is usually expected to 'have something to say' though it is always hard to explain what that 'something' is and how it is conveyed. The reason we need to hesitate about saying that self-expression does not necessarily imply communication is this: for an artist to feel that he has expressed himself, he must have some sense of satisfaction in what he has made; he must have achieved in it some understanding or brought some order out of disorder. His satisfaction, we could say, arises from the fact that he has communicated something *to himself*: he has succeeded in articulating something *out there* which was previously inarticulate *in here*. And if he has succeeded in making something that gives him satisfaction, that is self-reflexive, that 'says something' to him or for him, the chances are – human beings after all sharing the same common humanity – that it will communicate to and for others as well. Organizing language for others (communication) and organizing it for ourselves (self-expression) are not fundamentally different kinds of activity. However novel what a writer may struggle to express, however private and idiosyncratic his vision, however much he may have to forge a new way of saying it, he is still operating within and adapting to his own purposes a system of language and convention which is public. In practice, much of children's creative writing will oscillate rapidly between self-reflexive recalling and savouring and shaping of private experience and an audience-conscious attempt to tell, explain, describe, and yet it can still have a real unity. It is dangerous, therefore, to place too much emphasis on either communication or self-expression. To emphasize expression is to neglect the many ways we use language to participate in our society and stressing communication tends to suggest the transmission of pre-formulated messages and underestimates the extent to which we discover and understand in the actual process of matching words to experience.

In an earlier chapter on the development of English as a subject, I showed how, during the 1920s, a romantic and sometimes incautiously expressed faith in the creative, expressive, artistic abilities of children was followed by a reaction which lasted until after the Second World War. By 1927, writers like H.A. Treble were pouring scorn on the idea that children's writing could be seriously compared to that of mature artists and denouncing as lunacy and dereliction of duty the encouragement of unfettered self-expression from miniature selves who could have nothing significant to express rather than the cultivation of useful skills. The debate of more recent years has avoided these extremes but is still alive. Whenever there is publicly expressed anxiety about standards of literacy, understandably an accusing finger tends to be pointed at creative and imaginative work in schools. Some scepticism, too, has been voiced about how free and how genuinely self-expressive much of the work that goes under these labels really is. There are frequent misunderstandings: what is often called 'free writing' is not, of course, free in the sense that the teacher tells his pupils to write whatever they like. That would be to give the great majority far more freedom than they could handle. Rather it is free in the sense that the teacher having designated an area or theme and begun to explore it with the class in discussion or produced some stimulus material, words, music or pictures, leaves the class to follow it up or respond to it by writing in any way or form they choose. The teacher provides a springboard for the children's imaginations without defining the direction or duration of their flights.

The sceptic may still question whether he doesn't, in effect, stay on board as a kind of ghostly automatic pilot. Aren't children, anxious to please or simply desiring a quiet life, likely to play the sedulous ape? It is a legitimate doubt. Certainly, one sometimes sees children's work on show where one suspects that the feeling style is not the pupils' own but what they think the teacher wants. Good teachers, sensitive to this real danger, will develop a relationship with their classes which reduces the chances of this happening. Sensitive teachers, too, will not be constantly seeking to betray children into revealing what goes on in 'the foul rag-and-bone shop' of the heart. An excess to which the 'self-expression' approach may have been prone is an impertinently persistent probing of the depths of the psyche encouraged by an interest in various schools of psychoanalysis. The assurance for the children of a sympathetic and tactful reader of their writing which may sometimes be intensely personal, introspective and consciously or unconsciously self-revealing is one admirable thing, but for the teacher to persistently strive for that kind of writing when there may be no felt need for it is quite another. Geoffrey Willans in *Down With Skool* scores a palpable hit when he makes Molesworth Minor regret the time before English masters became 'ADVANCED chiz' and set straightforward essay topics like 'Wot i did in the hols'. '... In the good old days you knew where you were but now they are trying to read your inmost thorts heaven help them.'

There is no reason why much of children's writing should not be outwardly exploratory, inventive, imitative, playful or light-hearted and concerned with the world of ideas as well as feelings. After all, a worthwhile topic or stimulus material will stimulate thought as well as feeling; and this is not to deny the centrality of the child's own experience. American observers of English teaching in our schools in the late 1960s detected a certain anti-intellectualism, an emphasis on the affective at the expense of the cognitive which they probably rightly attributed to a reaction against past excesses in the opposite direction.

The sort of self-expression, then, which is central to an English teacher's job must not be too narrowly defined. It will be concerned with the whole self, actions and information, speculations and reflections as well as with feelings. At its best it will be manifestly an instrument of growth, of self-discovery and self-control because it is self-reflexive rather than merely self-reactive and because it is self-reflexive it will increase the ability both to communicate with and respond to other selves. It will produce writing and speech which deserves the respectful attention and constructive criticism of the teacher as the product of another growing mind and self and not as a reflection of his own.

IMAGINATION, CREATIVITY AND SELF-EXPRESSION

Suggested further reading

BUBER, M. (1961) *Between Man and Man* (Ch. 3) Fontana

CHARLTON, K. (1967) *Imagination and Education* University of Birmingham

FRYE, N. (1964) *The Educated Imagination* Indiana University Press

FURLONG, E.J. (1961) *Imagination* Allen and Unwin

HUDSON, L. (1966) *Contrary Imaginations* Methuen

JACKSON, P.W. and MESSICK, S. (1971) *The Person, the Product and the Response: Conceptual Problems in the Assessment of Creativity* Ch. 7 in *Personality, Growth and Learning* Longman/Open University

ROSS, M. (1975) *Arts and the Adolescent* Schools Council Working Paper 54 Evans/Methuen Educational

RUGG, H. (1963) *Imagination* Harper Row

RYLE, G. (1963) *The Concept of Mind* (Ch. 8) Penguin

SUTHERLAND, M.B. (1971) *Everyday Imagination and Education* Routledge & Kegan Paul

TORRANCE, E.P. (1962) *Guiding Creative Talent* Prentice Hall

VERNON, P.E. (1970) *Creativity* Penguin Modern Psychology Readings

WARNOCK, M. (1976) *Imagination* Faber

WHITEHEAD, F. (1970) *Creative Experiment: Writing and the Teacher* Chatto & Windus

WITKIN, R.W. (1974) *The Intelligence of Feeling* Heinemann

Creativity and Intelligence Section 6 in *Personality and Learning I* Hodder and Stoughton/Open University 1975

Postscript

One of the problems of writing a book about English is the necessity of breaking down a large and complex subject into chapters or sections without losing sight of its essential unity. By focusing on a score or so of questions I have made no bid to solve that problem and it would be absurdly ambitious to suppose one could neatly weave together again in a brief postscript all the strands that have been teased apart. I do think it is important for an English teacher to have a sense of the unity of his subject which holds together and keeps in balance the various activities – all worthwhile in themselves – which go on in English lessons. If English is fragmented into unrelated lessons and the teacher does not have a clear sense of what is central and what peripheral, he and his subject are peculiarly vulnerable at a time of reorganization and integration of the curriculum. This is not to suggest, of course, that the English department in a school should isolate itself in a defensive posture. I have argued (chapters 3, 5 and 6) that English should be the legitimate and indeed, essential concern of all teachers, that schools do need a language policy across the curriculum and that there is much to be gained from closer cooperation with teachers of social studies and the humanities. There remain large areas – the teaching of literature as literature and not an illustration of something else, the handling of children's personal creative writing – which are properly the province of specialist English teachers. And just because English is concerned with the children's growing awareness of themselves and their world it is constantly drawing on and integrating in fresh patterns of personal experience, material from other school disciplines.

I do not think there is one right way of teaching English nor that one English teacher is likely to be equally good at teaching all the different aspects of his subject. I think it understandable and probably healthy that there will be significant differences of emphasis when English teachers try to define what is central to their subject. Few today would want to revive the old notion that the core is a body of *knowledge about* language and literature though, incidentally, one hopes much useful, interesting and liberating knowledge will be transmitted. Whether one thinks of the core of English primarily in terms of the development of skills of communication in a contemporary social setting, the promotion of personal intellectual and emotional growth through articulating first-hand experience, exposure to the civilizing and sensitizing influence of great literature or developing powers of analysis and discrimination in respect of language in general and the mass media in particular is, perhaps, unimportant. Personally, I suspect that I swither between these and other ways of defining what is central from day to day and even from hour to hour of the school day. All involve thought and feeling, self and others, expression and communication, language and literature. All are important.

Common sense suggests that salvation lies in relating rather than separating and one can only feel saddened when one sees mutual misunderstanding and censoriousness between teachers one admires. Even sadder is a crippling pessimism about all aspects of contemporary culture and disgust with the way the world wags. Wordsworth could be pessimistic and censorious about his own times in which he saw 'a multitude of causes, unknown to former times ... acting with a combined force to blunt the discriminating powers of the mind' and generating a 'degrading thirst after outrageous stimulation' – words from the Preface to the *Lyrical Ballads* with a remarkably modern ring to them. But it is Wordsworth the poet of *The Excursion* who gives a positive and sustaining credo; 'We live by admiration, hope and love'. We must think first of the children we teach as living now and of their education as a live and lively part of that living in today's world. If we think too much of some probably mythical better yesterday or of them as citizens of tomorrow, we fail to make that live contact, we get it wrong,

For the new locus is never
Hidden inside the old one
Where Reason could rout it out,
Nor guarded by dragons in distant

Mountains where Imagination
Could explore it.'

(W.H. Auden: *The Age of Anxiety*)

The unity of English lies, I think, in making connections in practice while being aware of distinctions in theory. The experience of children is central and that which scholarship may progressively differentiate is existentially united in that living experience. The most obvious dichotomies in talk about the teaching of English, as we have seen, are language and literature; the spoken word and the written; reading and writing; reading that is literature and reading that is not; expression and communication; the language of thought and the language of feeling, and so on. At each point my discussion has implied in practice a pulling together rather than a holding apart of these antinomies.

Language and literature

The language of the classroom is the children's own spoken and written words and such words of others as can speak to them memorably at their stage of development. Both are indispensable. Literature brings in new voices, new experience and marvellous examples of the possibilities of language. If there has been a tendency in recent years to stress the centrality of the children's articulation of their own first-hand experience, this is because English was for decades hag-ridden by literature, the wrong literature presented at the wrong time and studied in the wrong way. When I started teaching in secondary schools nearly thirty years ago the books for second-year pupils from which I had to choose included Kinglake's *Eothen*, Read's *The Cloister and the Hearth*, Lamb's *Essays of Elia*, Conrad's *The Mirror of the Sea* and Stevenson's *Travels with a Donkey* – splendid books, no doubt – but for twelve-year-olds grotesque reach-me-downs from pre-war school certificate syllabuses. At the end of the year the senior English master set an examination testing the class's knowledge of the three texts I had elected to study with them. Many teachers of my generation could tell a similar story. English language study was separately examined and G.A. Twentyman's *English Grammar and Composition*, published in 1911, was the obligatory text.

Spoken and written words

Speaking comes before writing in every sense; in human history, in personal development, in quantity and importance in our relations with others: we learn it without conscious effort or formal teaching. It comes first, too, particularly for children, in the sense that before they can write about a subject they need to explore it and begin to order their ideas in the more informal, provisional and tentative language of speech. The best writing, too, for nearly every purpose, utilitarian or poetic, is 'a selection of language really used by men', language which has not grown awkward on the tongue or alien to the ear.

Reading and writing are obviously complementary activities in the same way. All our writing is to be read by someone (even if, sometimes, only by ourselves at some future date) but that 'someone' will normally be the whole class rather than just the teacher-marker. Most of it will be 'published' in some way within the classroom and some of it typed, duplicated and distributed more widely. Similarly, our reading will often lead into or grow out of what we choose to write about and all the time our experience of reading is building up our language resources for writing and talking.

Reading that is literature and reading that is not

Literature is read first for enjoyment rather than information, self-improvement or anything else and it involves an alert, attentive reading-to-realize-ourselves rather than an escapist reading-to-forget-ourselves. Today we know that nearly 30 per cent of twelve-year-olds never read a book outside school and the proportion increases with age. Those who do still read books tend to make a sharp distinction between Eng. Lit. on the one hand, for which they have some derogatory adjectives, and the reading-for-pleasure which any normal child would engage in voluntarily. The fault is that of adults; of parents and relatives for continuing to give children mainly Victorian classics rather than more up-to-date and attractive children's books of quality, and of teachers and examiners for requiring the premature study of great works which were, after all, written often long ago for adult readers. We know that the most important single factor which influences children's reading habits is what books are readily available: public libraries are often enlightened in this respect but relatively powerless without the active help of parents and teachers.

Much depends on acquiring the habit of reading for pleasure at the right age however omnivorous the fare. We have evidence that literary quality as recognized by sophisticated adults matters little to children as compared with features of the stories themselves which satisfy their emotional needs. There are two schools of thought here: on the one hand, purists who believe children should only be given poems, plays and stories of the highest literary quality selected and, if necessary, adapted to make them acceptable; on the other side are those who feel that one can better influence the development of individual taste by taking an interest in what is currently giving pleasure and seeking, a little at a time, to influence choice towards a wider range and higher quality of books which are enjoyed. This approach could be summarised in Caldwell Cook's words as 'the active philosophy of making pleasurable pursuits profitable'. Thinking back over the way in which my own taste developed – in painting and music as well as literature – I incline towards the latter view. So did A.J. Jenkinson in his survey *What Do Boys and Girls Read* in 1940: 'the policy of giving to schoolchildren only the best in literature involves a neglect of their own (childish) interests, produces bad teaching and unreal learning, and fails to contribute to the development of these interests into grown up interests'.

Salvation lies as ever in sensible compromise. There are undoubted masterpieces which are accessible to children but there is also a wealth of good books which may not be literature by any exacting standard but can nevertheless provide worthwhile imaginative experience for children and still retain the respect of teachers. An important part of the literature of the classroom too, will be the children's (and teacher's) own writing; and by writing, reading and discussing each other's writing, they will begin to develop as critics, finding out what one can look for, ask and say about words in action.

Expression and communication

Every instance of communication signifies that some act of expression has been received. Even the self-expression of 'the proud man apart' is articulating something 'out there' which was previously inarticulate 'in here'. To that extent he is communicating something to himself which is potentially accessible to other human beings even if that was no part of his intention. Self-expression which says nothing to sympathetically attentive others is unlikely to be self-expressive in the best, self-reflexive sense of the word.

The language of thought and the language of feeling

In their handbook *The Teaching of English* (1966) the Incorporated Association of Assistant Masters in Secondary Schools defined the aim of the English teacher as 'to increase the power of his pupils over language which deals with ideas, and to increase their power over language which expresses feelings'. It looks like another statement of duality at the heart of the subject. Of course, the pursuit of the first of these aims in stressing logical, rational, analytical thinking *could* encourage a clear, sceptical head at the expense of a hard heart and resistance to fictions and all emotive language including most literature. Similarly, emphasis on the culture of the feelings *could* lead to a careless contempt for reason and logical consistency. There is a source for conflict and tension here in English teaching, as in life, but to make it an issue on which one could take sides in a pedagogical debate would surely be to close our eyes to the complexity of the human condition. It is feeling, Shaw said, which makes a man think but, equally, ideas can rouse passions and modify sensibility. We do not live by reason alone or by imagination. The wise man is not ruled by his head or his heart but must listen to both and reconcile their promptings. Imaginative literature is the great unifier: it provides the finest record of what men have thought and felt and the subtlest exploration of the relationship of head and heart in human experience. This is the sense in which it is and must remain central to English teaching. The enmity which Plato pictured between intellect and imagination becomes the most dangerous legacy of the Greeks to Western civilization if we forget that they were really reconciled in his own life and work: he would have been banished and his book banned in a Republic where Philosopher-kings proscribed poetry.

There are, of course, many other apparent dualities in talk about English teaching and some of them such as poetry and prose, appreciation of and knowledge about literature, critical skills and creative ones have been discussed earlier and need not be re-opened here. If it is true that the unity of English is one in which all these parts have to be held harmoniously in balance, what gives English its overall integrity is the individual pupil's growing and changing need for language to come to terms with himself and the world around him. This is the sense in which English can be properly thought of as child-centred and it properly limits the sense in which literature, too, can be said to be central.

As we said early on, English is not in many ways comparable to most other subjects, least of all to 'linear', incremental ones like mathematics, science or modern languages where one step in learning, comprehension or skill necessarily precedes the next. The early stages of learning language skills in one's native tongue *do* take place in an orderly sequence in all normal human beings and they have been mapped out in some detail but they are all behind us before we ever come to school. Whether we turn to linguistics or to literary criticism we shall find no agreement about the internal structure or 'discipline' of English. There is no necessary informational core and no logic to give structure to a syllabus. The young teacher can feel very insecure. He is told to respond to and stimulate the interests and language needs of his pupils and somehow to enrich their lives with no orderly sequence of prescribed work to lean on. He cannot simply adopt another teacher's scheme of work; it has got to be right for him and his class. Principles which give coherence to the syllabuses of other subjects such as tackling the simple before the complex, concrete before abstract, regular before irregular, common before uncommon, earlier before later, close-at-hand before distant, and so on, are of very limited help to him and sometimes positively misleading. This is why he needs, perhaps more than any other teacher, a philosophy of his subject such as this book may have begun to sketch out for him. He needs, too, the constant support of more experienced colleagues while he begins day by day to translate that philosophy into classroom activity and develop his own style as a teacher.

If there are principles of structure and development in his subject they are to be sought in patterns of human growth, physical, intellectual, emotional, social, spiritual, rather than in his subject matter. Of course children change and develop over the period of their secondary schooling; they change from children into adults or near-adults. The way that 'power over language which deals with ideas ... and ... expresses feelings' develops as part of that growth is not easily observable or measurable in the short term because it is not separable from the process of maturation itself. Maturity, except in the physical sense, is a vague notion which we use and interpret according to our own values. One thing is sure: it is a slow process.

How would I indicate the changes which, as an English teacher, I would value and therefore hope to see and promote in due time? They might be listed as follows: the ability to match language appropriately to an increasing variety of situations and purposes; a growing capacity for symbolic thinking, for handling abstractions and figurative language alongside *but not replacing* forceful use of the concrete and the literal; likes and dislikes becoming less impermanent and intuitive and better articulated and supported with reasons; taste in reading becoming both more catholic and more discriminating with a growing sense of the historical context of individual books; argument, including the ability to listen to and take account of other points of view, developing out of assertion and counter assertion; an increasing self-expressiveness and individuality of style. Embracing all the others, I would hope to see in my pupils an increasing enjoyment of language, adventurousness in using it and self-confidence that they could communicate effectively in speech and writing and read or listen with understanding.

Do I hear someone mutter, 'Pigs might fly?' or see that politely knowing look which says so eloquently, 'I suppose he's paid to have his head in the clouds'. Well, of course there is an air of unreality about any statement of aims, goals, ideals when one is confronted by the apparently ineluctable apathy and obdurate illiteracy of some classes but what alternative to believing that silk purses can and do grow out of sows' ears does the teacher have, apart from sinking into apathy himself? He should draw up his own list of desirable changes rather than accept mine. If he is wise he will not expect to achieve them quickly or necessarily pursue them directly. The short-term behavioural objectives so useful to other teachers will be little help to him, concerned as he is with the affective as much as the cognitive and with such relative intangibles as 'appreciation', 'response', 'discrimination', 'sensibility' and 'self-knowledge'. Patterns of development will be as numerous as the developing individuals and, as Frank Whitehead puts it, 'decisive are the amount and quality of the linguistic experience provided by the child's social environment, the relationships he forms with other people, and the pressures from within which move him to use language to satisfy his human needs'. (*Use of English XXII* 1.p.6) The teacher cannot do everything. He cannot expect the reassurance of hard evidence week by week or term by term that he is getting anywhere. He must have faith that plenty of enjoyable reading, writing, talking and listening arising out of present interest are enriching that linguistic environment and stirring those inward pressures to express and to communicate.

Index

Names of authors rather than titles of books are included since, in the text, the latter are not mentioned without the former.

Abbs, P. 28
accidence, 39
Adams, A. 28
Addison, J. 15
Alfred the Great, 7
Anglist/Anglistics, 9
Anglo-Saxon, 7, 13, 39, 40, 43, 56, 82
appreciation, 77–81
Aristotle, 70–1, 95
Arnold, M. 14, 20, 70, 95
Ascham, R. 13
Ashton-Warner, Sylvia 122
Auden, W. H. 98, 133

Bacon, Sir Francis 108
Bagnall, N. 28
Balchin, W. G. V. 50
Ballard, P. B. 18, 21
Bantock, G. H. 58
Barnes, D. 58
Bartlett, F. C. 112
basic skills, 49–53
Bateson, F. W. 77, 89
Benfer, M. C. 55
Bennett, A. 100
Berkeley, G. 111
Blake, W. 73
Blishen, E. 12
Board of Education, 14
Boas, George 71
Boethius, 7
Brett, R. L. 103
Bridges, R. 93
BBC 69
Britton, J. 58, 81
Buber, M. 121, 130
Bullock Report, *A Language for Life* (1975), 26, 28, 52

Catherwood, C. 55
Caxton, W. 42
Chaucer, G. 7, 14, 42, 82, 85
Charlton, K. 130
Chesterton, G. K. 68
child-centred education, 19, 137
Children's Reading Interests (1975), 67
Chinese, 7, 38, 39
Churchill, W. 14
Cizek, F. 21
Cobbett, W. 53
Coleridge, S. T. 21, 74, 80, 99, 111–3, 116–7
Colet, J. 63
Collingwood, R. G. 107–8
communication, 126–30, 135–6
comprehension, 78–80
Conrad, J. 133
Cook, H. Caldwell, 15, 18, 119, 135
Craig, D. 28
creativity/creative writing, 15–7, 20–1, 81, 91, 107, 109, 112, 116–30
Creber, J. W. P. 28, 58, 107
criticism, 16, 65–7, 72, 78–82, 90–2, 120–1, 137

Crowther Report (1959), 49, 89
Cymric, 37

Daiches, D. 103
Dante, 65
Darbyshire, A. E. 58
Davies, H. S. 58
dialect, 7, 8, 19, 42–4, 46, 58
Dieth, E. 43
Dixon, J. 10, 28
Doughty, A. & P. 58–9
drama, 22, 81–2, 108, 110, 119, 125
Drever, J. 113
Dryden, J. 7, 75, 82, 90, 112

Elia, Essays of 15
Eliot, T. S. 16, 78, 95, 100, 104
Elyot, Sir Thomas, 13
English: accent 42, 43, 58
  American 43
  and social class 47–8
  as a foreign language 7, 38
  as a subject 11–22
  as a verb 7
  as a world language 8
  'bad' English 7
  basic English 38
  bilingualism in 46–8
  diphthongs 40
  etymology 58
  'good' English see Standard English
  phonology 39–40
  pidgin 38
  pronunciation 8, 40, 42–4, 46
  remedial 27
  specialist in 9–10
  spoken 18, 33, 50, 119
  Standard (correct, good) 8, 19, 41–8, 119
  syllabus 11, 131, 137
  unity of 131–9
  vocabulary 37–9, 43–4, 57
  vowels 40
  word order 39
Empson, W. 16
Eskimo, 38
Esperanto, 8
examinations, 13, 15–6, 18–9, 23, 54, 56, 65, 73, 77, 79, 87–92, 101
explication, 79

figures of speech, 15
Fisher, H. A. L. 88
Flower, F. D. 58
free writing, 128–9
French, 11, 33, 35, 37–8, 40, 42
Freud, S. 71
Frisian, 37
Fromm, E. 122
Frost, R. 76, 108
Frye, N. 130
Furlong, E. J. 130

German, 35, 37, 39–40, 56
Goethe, 65
grammar, 13–5, 18–9, 27, 39, 44, 54–7, 119
Graves, R. 101, 122
Greek, 39, 56, 71, 95, 136
Gutenberg, Johannes, 50

Hadow Report (1926), 19
Halliday, F. E. 59
Halliday, M. A. K. 46, 59
handwriting, 14
Harding, D. W. 104
Hardy, Thomas, 94
Hartog, Philip, 15
Hazlitt, W. 82
Heinemann, M. 28
Henley,,W. E. 14
Hobbes, T. 112
Hoggart, R. 20
Holbrook, D. 22, 28
Holmes, Edmund, 15, 18
Homer, 65
homonyms, 38
homophones, 38
Horace, 70
Hourd, M. 21
Housman, A. E. 95, 97

Hudson, L. 130
Hume, D. 65–6

imagination, 107–16, 136
Incorporated Association of
Assistant Masters, 16, 103, 136
Indo-European, 37, 39
Initial Teaching Alphabet, 40
integration, 14, 17, 28, 131
Italian, 37

Jackson,,P. W. 130
James, W. 12
Jenkinson, A. J. 135
Jesperson, Otto, 14, 37–8
Joyce, James, 76
Johnson, S. 85, 96, 101, 108, 114
Jonson, B. 94

Kant, I. 110–1, 117
Keats, J. 83
Kekulé, August, 109
Ker, W. P. 90
Kinglake, A. W. 133
Knights, L. C. 76, 88

Lamb, Charles, 133
Lamborn, E. A. Greening, 16
Language: Some Suggestions for Teachers of English and Others (1954), 54–5
Laski, M. 97
Latin, 11, 13, 33, 39, 55–6, 71
Lawrence, D. H. 94, 97
Lawton, D. 59
Lear, E. 101
Leavis, F. R. 16, 20, 23, 72, 104
Lewis, C. Day, 98, 104, 127
Lewis, C. S. 24, 68, 75, 104
Lewis, R. T. 14
lexis, see English vocabulary
linguistics, 18–9, 23, 48, 54, 137
literacy/illiteracy, 7, 14, 18, 26, 33, 49–54, 118, 128
Locke, J. 111
Lockwood Report (Eighth Report of Secondary Schools Examination Council, 1964) 54, 88
Longinus, 96

Macaulay, Lord, 15
Macaulay, W. J. 55
McIntosh, A. 46, 59
MacLeish, A. 24
Marland, M. 28–9
Mass Media, 20, 33, 44, 46, 49–50, 69, 116, 132
Mathieson, M. 29
Maugham, W. Somerset, 96
Mayhead, R. 104
'mediacy', 49
Messick, S. 130
Mill, J. S. 74, 112–3
Milton, J. 14, 65, 97
Montague, C. E. 98
morality, 70–5, 98, 113, 116–7
Morris, N. 20
Mulcaster, R. 13

National Association for the Teaching of English, 22
Neill, A. S. 82
Nesfield, J. C. 14
Newbolt Report (1921), 15, 20, 26, 70, 87
Newman, J. H. 66
Newsom Report (1963), 18–9, 119
Niblett, W. R. 66
Norse, 43
Northern Universities Joint Matriculation Board, 89
Norwood Report (1941) 88
numeracy, 49–50
Nunn, Sir Percy, 15, 119–20

Ogden, C. K. 38
Old English see Anglo-Saxon
Oliphant, Mrs. M. 114
oracy, 18, 50
Ortega y Gasset, 95
orthography see spelling
Orton, H. 43
Owen, Dorothy Tudor, 15

Owens, G. 29
Oxford English Dictionary, 9, 13

Palmer, D. J. 29
Palser, E. M. 14
Pater, W. 82
Peel, M. 104
Phenix, P. M. 11
phoneme, 39–40
Plato, 70, 136
Plowden Report (1967) 19
poetry, 93–100
Pope, A. 7, 22, 82, 101
Potter, Simeon, 59
Potter, Stephen, 79, 85, 104
practical criticism, 79–80, 90, 92
Pressey, S. L. 56
prose, 93–100
punctuation, 21, 27, 45, 119

Quirk, R. 54, 59

Read, C. 133
Read, H. 21
reading (children's habits & tastes) 13, 80, 133–5
Reeves, J. 104
recitation, 14, 101–3
register, 19, 23, 41
Rice, J. M. 55
Richards, I. A. 16, 38, 72–3, 82, 100, 104
Robinson, I. 120
Ross, M. 130
Rowe, A. 29
Rugg, H. 130
Russian, 7, 39, 56
Ryle, G. 130

Saintsbury, G. 82
Sampson, G. 15, 18, 41, 73
Sanskrit, 34
Sartre, J. P. 10
Saunders, M. 29
Schools Council Working Paper No. 52, 67
Scrutiny, 20, 88
self expression, 16, 17, 58, 117, 125–30, 135–6
semiotics, 34
Shaw, B. 43, 136
Shakespeare, W. 14, 67, 71, 82, 85, 103, 109
Shayer, D. 22, 29
Shipley, J. 93, 104
Sidney, Sir P. 93
Skelton, R. 104
Slade, P. 22
Snow, C. P. 50
social studies, 20, 24, 131
sociology, 48
Sonnenschein, E. A. 14
Sophocles, 65
Spanish, 7, 37
spelling, 14, 21, 27, 38, 40, 45, 119
Spender, S. 99, 112–3
Spens Report (1938) 19
Spenser, E. 13, 65, 82
Spinosa, 74
Squire, J. R. 29
Stevens, R. 104
Stevenson, R. L. 133
Stratta, L. 29
Strevens, P. 46, 59
Stuart, S. 22
Stubbs, M. 59
Style, 41
Sutherland, M. B. 130
symbol, 33–6
syntax, 39

taste, 64–5
Taylor, C. W. 119
Teaching of English in England, The (1921) see Newbolt Report
Thomas, E. 76
Thompson, D. 16, 104
Thorndike, E. L. 14
Thornton, G. 59
Tolstoy, L. 65
Tomkinson, W. S. 16
Torrance, E. P. 130
Treble, H. A. 128
Trim, J. L. M. 47

Trudgill, [illegible]
Twentyman, G. A. [illegible], 135

UNESCO 51–2
Use of English, The 22, 139
Verity, A. W. 71
Vernon, P. E. 130
'videacy'/visual literacy, 50
Viola, W. 21
Volapuk, 8

Walsh, W. 104
Warnock, M. 130
Warren, A. 104
Watts, A. F. 18
Wellek, R. 104
Welsh, 37
Whitehead, F. 29, 89, 124, 130, 139
Wilbur, R. 127
Wilkinson, A. 29, 41, 59
Willan,,G. 10, 129
Williams, R. 122
Wiseman, S. 92
Witkin, R. W. 130
Wordsworth, W. 10, 21, 74, 93, 95, 132

Yale Conference, 120